Masterpiece

IN THE

Making

*Become an Original
in a World of Imitations*

RUTH MITCHELL

Text: Ruth Mitchell
Cover and Interior Design and Layout: Danielle Smith-Boldt

ISBN 978-0-578-63174-5

ACKNOWLEDGMENTS

I would be remiss if I did not acknowledge that crafting a book cannot be done in a vacuum. I have been blessed through-out my life with people who believed in me and cheered me on. Some I have just met in the last few months including my editor, Angela Guzman, who so brilliantly captured the heart of this book and was gentle and yet firm with me on this project. My friends who have endured hearing about "my dream" for way more years than was normal and yet continued to believe in me and in the book. My parents Herb and Helen Selby who never allowed me to be anything less than the best God designed for me, believing in me and reassuring me from the very first attempt at creative writing in grade school to now. Thanks for your unconditional love and how you both demonstrate the love Jesus has for all of us through how you love one another and how you loved me. To each of my kids, Will, Brandon, Meghan and Renny thanks for allowing me to share some of our family "secrets" and help mold me into the woman I am today. And to my number one fan and champion of my heart, my husband Renny. Thanks, babe, for never ever giving up on me and kicking me in the rear when I was discouraged and did not believe this dream would ever become a reality. Thanks for your encouragement even when I did not receive it as that and for being the voice in my heart as I pushed through till the end. I love you and would not want to do this life without you by my side.

Your fellow Masterpiece in the Making,
Ruth

CONTENTS

PART ONE

Know
the Master

CHAPTER 1

Who Is The Master?

*"And as You speak a hundred billion creatures catch Your breath
evolving in pursuit of what You said"*

"So Will I" Hillsong United

God as Creator

Surrounded by verdant green and the soothing sounds of the river making its way over smooth stones, as the occasional fish breaks the surface to jump and splash, He stands and takes in the immenseness of His creation. He realizes, there is no one to take care of this creation. At that moment, the Master Creator decides He must put all of His efforts into creating the best of everything He created. He knew the only one capable of caring for His creation was someone who had His own imagination, creativity, heart and love: thus, man and woman were created.

Humans were created in the very image of the Artist and designed from the beginning of time, to have purpose and relationship with our Creator and each other. Created by His breath, His most prized of all creation. We were not just declared good, but very good.

God spoke: "Let us make human beings in our image, make them reflecting our nature...God created human beings; he created them godlike, Reflecting God's nature. He created them male and female" (Gen 1:26,27 MSG)

Unlike any of His other creations, man and woman had a relationship with the Artist interwoven into the fabric of their being. We were created to be creative, as this is where we find our significance, because we carry the DNA of the Master and by our very design need to create a life of meaning and purpose. The longing every human has for significance is designed and created by God. The desire to design, create and fill the world with beauty is derived from the essence of God each of us carries. To know and be known is the innermost desire as a human is the direct result of being made in the image of God.

It is the challenge of every human to live in that purpose. When we try to live our lives outside of understanding who we are, we face failure, disappointment and lack of fulfillment. Our world is full of people who seem to have it all and have done it all, yet they are the unhappiest and least fulfilled people I know. When we learn to live with the deep knowledge within our soul of who God says we are, we live fulfilled, with a true sense of purpose and significance.

The bible utilizes the word "Master" as a word translated from the word "Lord" or the Hebrew word Adonay. Master is a term that indicates one of honor and authority, but it also implies the one you are addressing has mastered something and is worthy of our respect. When someone is a master at something, they have reached the pinnacle of accomplishment. A master carpenter is not just someone who creates beautiful furniture and cabinets. In addition to producing woodwork, the master carpenter went through specific training and apprenticed with another carpenter.

Our Lord, Master by his very nature is a "Master Creator" and we are the object of His creative nature and His greatest masterpiece.

If we are His greatest work, what is our response? What is our obligation? What should this stir in our hearts and how can we live up to our full potential?

God as Lover of My Soul

For as long as I can remember I have heard the words, "God loves you and has a wonderful plan for your life." For many years, I focused on the second half of that statement and did not really grasp the first part. What does it mean to have "an understanding" for the love of the Creator of the universe? Who is this Creator and why does He love me?

"Daddy, daddy dance with me," I cried out as my father walked into the living room weary from work. Without hesitation, he scooped me up into his arms and we danced there in the living room, with only the music of our hearts to keep time. His strong arms held me in an embrace without a care in the world I understood when I was in his arms, I was safe and secure. The outside world did not exist, it was just daddy and me. He slowly twirled me until I was dizzy, and we giggled as we dropped to the floor. I laid my head on his chest, I felt the rhythmic beat of his heart - I knew I was loved, safe and cherished.

As a child, I never doubted God's love for me. I was one of the lucky/blessed ones. My daddy was kind and gentle yet, strong and he never failed to let me know how precious I was. As I grew up, life happened and doubt crept in. As I got older other voices began to be louder and more important. Not only did the voice of God fade into the background, so did my own voice.

*Then Jesus said, "Believe me when I tell you that anyone who does not enter the sheepfold though the door, but climbs in by some other way, is a thief and a rogue. It is the shepherd of the flock who goes in by the door. It is to him the door-keeper opens the door and it is his voice that the sheep **recognize**. He calls his own sheep by name and leads them out of the fold, and when he has driven all his own flock outside, he goes in front of them himself, and the sheep follow him because they know his voice. They will never follow a stranger— indeed, they will run away from him, for they do not recognize strange voices"* (John 10: 1-5).

Doubt found its voice in my head. I began to take His love for granted and I no longer guarded the heart that was so graciously given. I gave credence to the outside voices - voices of my teachers, my peers, my bosses and even my friends. Voices that convinced me I wasn't good enough or that I thought too highly of myself.

It wasn't just the voices, but circumstances as well, allowing me to believe lies about myself and the One who loved me the most. How had I allowed those voices to have more weight, more credence, than the One who made me? Even as I am writing, there is a voice that I still battle with in my head.

"Ruth, please tell me that your baby brother wrote this paper, it is one of the worst papers you have ever written," said my 12th grade English teacher.

My face flushed with embarrassment, as 20 pairs of my peers' eyes stared at me in shock. *Did she really just say that out loud?* Tears threatened to overflow, furthering my shame. There was no kindness in her words, only biting sarcasm and criticism. Grabbing the paper from my teacher, I fled the room. Tears blinded my eyes as I rushed into my counselor's office to drop the class, avoiding further humiliation.

My English teacher's loud voice still rings in my head today. I must silence that voice with many of my blog posts, emails and even some texts I write - even now as I put keyboard to paper.

There is a second voice that follows after I hear her voice. It is an all too familiar one.

"Of course, you can't write! Who are you to think that anything you write is good enough? Who do you think will ever want to read what you write?"

Unfortunately, that second voice sounds very much like my own. I learned the second voice is just an imitation of mine and not truly my own. I have chosen to ignore the voices threatening my creativity and desire to share how loved we are by our Creator.

It wasn't until my early 30s, when I came to grips with some of the voices I had invited in and the power I'd given them. It was at a time of personal crisis when a dear friend challenged me to have a different view - to fall in love again with the One who created me. I had to dig back into who and what made up the One who loved me most. I had to learn all over again, to hear the voice of the One called out to me for relationship, and to learn what the meaning of God as the "lover of my soul."

During this time, I learned the discipline of solitude - which believe me, for this extreme extravert was excruciating. I had to learn to sit and be quiet, to look to what I knew about Jesus, Father God and most importantly the Holy Spirit. I had to develop a new relationship with God. I looked back to the little girl who had no problem sitting on her father's lap, both literally and figuratively.

It was during one particular time of solitude that my Heavenly Father brought me back to that place. He reminded me of His desire to dance with me, to cherish me and make me feel safe.

"The Lord your God is in the midst of you, a Mighty One, a Savior [Who saves]! He will rejoice over you with joy; He will rest [in silent satisfaction] and in His love He will be silent and make no mention [of past sins, or even recall them]; He will exult over you with singing" (Zeph 3:17 AMPC).

The word "exult" is rooted in the Hebrew word which means to spin around under violent emotions - if that doesn't describe dancing, I am not sure what does. As I got back to that place, my heart expanded, and my doubts and fears slowly subsided. I still need to remind myself of His outrageous love for me, even as I type these words, my heart again swells with His love.

There is a big difference in my heart, when I realize that He will be silent about my past sins. Who can be capable of this but a good God? The character of a forgiving and loving God! He forgives when we cannot forgive ourselves.

Every human being has a deep desire for two things: significance and to be loved. I believe this comes from the DNA of our Master Creator. In order to understand our significance, we need to understand first where the need to be loved originates.

*"I have loved you with an everlasting love, I have **drawn** you with unfailing kindness"* (Jeremiah 31:3). Emphasis mine.

This is what everyone has the desire to hear and know. When we believe that we were "drawn" or created in unfailing love and kindness, it changes everything. This Master Artist is full of love and compassion for His creation. I am not sure we can quite grasp his everlasting, unending love. A love that does not ask for anything in return, other than to receive. To be drawn by unfailing kindness.

If you have been alive for more than five minutes, someone has been unkind, has failed you and loved you with strings attached. Yet His love never runs out. Never is from the Greek word that means never. (Okay, so I made that part up.) The truth is never, truly, means never.

"We, though, are going to love-love and be loved. First we were loved, now we love. He loved us first""(1 John 4:19 Message).

On paper it is simple. We love because He first loved us. The hard part is receiving His love, giving it back to Him and giving to others. The only one in the equation who deserves to be loved is God, and yet He is the only one who does not need it.

"Drink deeply of the pleasures of this God. Experience for yourself the joyous mercies he gives to all who turn to hide themselves in him" (Psalm 34:8 Passion Translation).

As you turn the pages of this book, I believe you will discover who He is, and as a result discover who you are.

Psalm 37:4 says it best, "Delight yourselves also in the Lord, and he will give you the desires and secret petitions of your heart."

At the end of each chapter you will have the option to further your exploration of your design. You are a piece of art in progress. So, look at yourself as ART.

ASK: For you, what is the hardest part for you about believing you are God's best work?

_____

_____

READ: Read the creation story again and imagine what it would have been like to be in Adam and Eve's place. How does it make you feel to be called very good? (Genesis 1:1-31)

TELL: Tell yourself, even if you don't believe it yet, "I am His best work."

CHAPTER 2

Intimacy, The Scariest Word

"It is insanity to run from God and search for love."

–Erwin McManus, *Soul Cravings*

A cool breeze rustled through the trees as brilliant shades of colorful birds flitted from branch to branch. Dew still dripping from the grass as He walked silently on the fresh carpet of green, a majestic lion slowly crossing His path, so much life and so much peace all in one place. Yet, one thing was missing.

"Where are you?" He called out in this new game of hide and seek. "Adam, where are you?" the Master Creator called to His favorite creation.

"Why did you miss our morning appointment? I have longed to spend time with you in the cool of this magnificent day. Today we were going to explore more of my gift of creation to you and Eve."

"Where are you?" the Master Creator still calls today, and like Adam, we find ourselves hiding. Hiding for many personal reasons, but still hiding. Hiding under our blanket of shame. If He really knew me, how could He love me? Trying desperately to cover our nakedness so no one will see who we really are.

"Did God really say you could not eat from the tree of the knowledge of good and evil?" This still rings in our ears.

All relationships, whether human or divine, are based on one very vital component - trust. Trust allows us to be fully open with no fear of judgement or shame. From the beginning of time, intimacy's enemy has been broken trust.

The enemy of our soul continues to whisper in our ear. "Did He really say He loved you or is it just a means to an end?" The serpent's intent is to undermine the sweet, intimate relationship God desires, and which he designed from the beginning of time. The enemy of our soul introduced doubt into our finite human hearts. Our hearts are so fragile and yet, have the most power over us.

I have heard intimacy can be defined as "into me you see." The very thought of intimacy can cause a grown man to run out of the room screaming, or a confident woman to fall to the floor in tears. It is terrifying and yet, at the center of our being. Intimacy is one of our greatest human desires and can be considered a need- the desire to be fully known.

When we are fully known and loved, we are understood. My soul is satisfied, and I have the confidence to love others. So why is this such a scary thing? Why do men struggle to reveal their hearts? Why do women refuse to be loved wholly? The answer is two-fold; we are terrified of what we believe to be true of ourselves and we are naked and ashamed when God created us naked and unashamed.

My phone rang and my neighbor said, "Hi Ruth, how are you today?"

"I am doing well. The morning was a bit rough, as you know life with my three toddlers is certainly keeping me on my toes. I am still cleaning oatmeal off the ceiling from breakfast. Did Will make it to your house okay? I watched him walk across the street so, I assume he is okay." I asked.

"Yes, he is here safe and sound. But, did you know that Brandon is here too?" my neighbor answered with a concerned voice.

"Oh, my goodness, he must have gotten up from his nap, figured out how to open the lock on the front door, and snuck out without me even knowing."

I realized my almost two-year-old had escaped his room, stealthily opened our front door, crossed the street, and went three doors down. Clearly, it was time to put a different lock on the front door.

"I will be right down to get him as soon as I can. I will grab the baby and walk over," I assured my neighbor. "He always wants to be where his big brother is."

"Well, you might want to bring some of his clothes with you too. No need for shoes because he has his boots on," she replied.

"What?" I gasped.

My adventurous 22-month-old snuck out, crossed the street in his favorite pair of cowboy boots and forgot his clothes! He was completely naked except for those fancy grey cowboy boots. He was naked and unashamed.

When do we realize that our nakedness is something to cover and hide? I have terrifying memories of junior high showers. I was sure that I was the only one who felt this way. Shame in the color or should I say lack of color of my skin, and the shape, or again, lack of shape, of my body.

Nakedness without shame was God's original plan. There are no barriers between man and God or woman and God. They walked together in the cool of the day, exploring, talking and I believe dreaming of how to subdue and conquer the new and burgeoning world. It was not until they doubted who they were that shame entered the picture.

Like my son, who had no reason to feel shame over his physical nakedness, we are born with no reason to feel shame about our emotional nakedness. We were designed to be known intimately, without shame or concern. What causes us to doubt ourselves and our need for intimacy? Where does the doubt enter and prevent us from being naked and unashamed?

For me it was so subtle, and the barriers simply built up over the years. My relationship with God and with others was built on a belief, that everyone wanted to be my friend and wanted the best for me. My first broken heart came when my first BFF laughed at me while I was passionately signing my heart out.

"Oh, Ruth you are a terrible singer. Who do you think you are? Karen Carpenter?"

Now before you break out laughing, do the math and realize how old I really am. It was one of the first scrapes to the delicate skin of vulnerability.

The problem is with each untreated scrape or scratch, the wound can get bigger. We create protective barriers and do not truly allow anyone in. As I grew and felt the need to please others, I learned to pretend to be someone I was not. I would pretend that words and actions did not hurt me.

The summer before I turned 13, I found myself in the wrong place at the wrong time and someone that I trusted took advantage of me. I did not have the ability to say no. The wound was a much larger cut than I realized. I buried it deep, or so I thought. It wasn't until I was married that a huge doubt entered my mind concerning my relationship with my husband. I also questioned who God was and recognized that this wound created a barrier from fully being loved and accepted by God and my spouse.

My relationship with God started a very young age. in fact, at three I gave my heart and life to Jesus and never doubted His reality in my life. I knew that He loved me. I wasn't convinced that He really liked me. I remember singing a song that declared, "Jesus, lover of my soul, Jesus I will never let you go." The line declaring Jesus being the lover of my soul, felt shallow and trite. Did he really love my soul? Did he really care about who I was, or did He just need me to do things to help spread the word about Him? Oh, I knew there were *things* he liked about me, but did he just plain old like ME?

Over the last 25 years, I had the privilege to work with women and men who built barriers against hurt. As a result, the impenetrable wall preventing anyone in and keeping them from getting out. The stories are heartbreaking and horrendous. It is still hard for me to believe what humans can do to one another and do not consider how their actions affect others. I guess that is why it is called sin.

I would love to sit with each of you, to hear your story of love and hurt, victory and loss. Each of us have learned to construct those barriers and walls, which is why over 2000 years ago God said, "Enough is enough. I will tear down the wall between myself and my creation." The wall everyone is guilty of building, whether by design or default. This wall has become a prison keeping us from truly experiencing the intimacy we were all created to enjoy with our Creator. A wall once torn down, allowing us to walk in freedom, to be wholly loved, wholly known by our Creator and by others. It allows us to sing with confidence and understanding that Jesus truly is the lover of my soul. He knows me the best and loves me the most.

The cry of every soul, "See Me." The Creator who is LOVE, imparted that need into each one of us and until that need is fulfilled with Him, we will seek it in the wrong places. Drugs, sex, food, wrong relationships - and dare I even say shopping - are all desperate attempts to fill the void and numb the pain of loneliness that only can be filled when we trust the love our Creator.

How can we be seen, if we are too busy hiding? Many years ago, this game of hide and seek started in the garden. This dangerous and unfulfilling game leaves us empty and searching to fill up the chasm in our soul.

The amazing thing is God is in plain sight. He is waiting for you to simply open your eyes and see Him. How can we take off the blindfold that keeps us from relationship? How can we change the rules of engagement, albeit our rules not His? Rules that tell us we are not worthy, that he could never love anyone like you. If I let my guard down, my heart will be open to more hurt and disappointment. These are the rules the enemy of our soul has whispered in our ear from the beginning. But God never was the one hiding, it has always been us hiding from Him.

God, Creator of the heavens— he is, remember, God. Maker of earth— he put it on its foundations, built it from scratch. He didn't go to all that trouble to just leave it empty, nothing in it. He made it to be lived in. This God says: "I am God, the one and only. I don't just talk to myself or mumble under my breath. I never told Jacob, 'Seek me in emptiness, in dark nothingness.' **I am God. I work out in the open,** *saying what's right, setting things right. So gather around, come on in, all you refugees and castoffs"* (Isaiah 45:19).

God changed those rules when He sent Jesus to help us remove our blindfold, and sent the Holy Spirit to be our teammate. The Holy Spirit who counters the whisper with a shout of who you can become when in relationship with Jesus. The Holy Spirit whose name means breath of God who was there when you were created at the side of Father cheering you on from the very beginning.

"Look at this one Father, can't you see who she will become. I love her so much already. Wait till she realizes she was created to be loved and to love."

The Holy Spirit is our teammate, our champion and our cheerleader. His job is to help us relearn the rules of engagement, to relearn to walk in the cool of the day with our Creator. To learn the voice of the One who loves us most and teach us to trust once again. To trust when we do open up does not bring condemnation but healing, life and vitality.

Take some time to look at yourself as his ART:

ASK: God to reveal what part of yourself you are trying to hide from Him and what is hindering you from an intimate relationship with Jesus?

_____

_____

READ: *"Where could I go from with your Spirit? Where could I run and hide from your face? If I go up to heaven, you're there! If I go down to the realm of the dead, you're there too! If I fly with wings into the shining dawn, you're there! If I fly into the radiant sunset, you're there waiting! c Wherever I go, your hand will guide me; your strength will empower me. It's impossible to disappear from you or to ask the darkness to hide me, for your presence is everywhere, bringing light into my night"* (Psalms 139:7-11 TPT).

TELL: God an area you want him to heal in your heart and trust Him enough to no longer hide it from Him.

CHAPTER 3

Removing Barriers to Intimacy

*"Perhaps that's another reason true intimacy is so frightening.
It's the one thing we all want and must give up control to get."*

—Donald Miller, *Scary Close*

Why is it so hard to walk in intimacy with the one who knows you best? How is it we can skirt through life and never be wholly intimate with our Creator?

Back to the garden, the enemy of our soul does not want us to understand fully who we are because when we do, his very life is in danger. His whole agenda is to separate man from God and man from one another. He is the one who whispers in our ear, "Did God really say?" The subtle way in which he works creates that wedge which becomes a chasm if not dealt with.

Because we were born into Adam's family, we have inherited that same self-doubt. The enemy does not know your future, nor can he read your mind, but boy does he know your past and it is his favorite tool he keeps in his toolbox to use against us. The accuser wants us to believe that our *past* is what defines us. Enter the shame and blame which keep us from an intimate relationship with God.

Shame is the voice that says, "If God really knew what I have done or what has been done to me, He would not want a relationship with me." Shame is what keeps our secrets locked up tight inside our own head. Shame shuts down hopes and dreams, but also keeps us from believing we are enough. Shame stunts all growth and it is poison to our soul.

Shame is not the only tool in the box; blame is just as sharp an instrument. Blame says everything I have done or has been done to me is someone else's fault. Blame says if only that person had not done (fill in the blank), I could be more or do more or have ore. Blame says my poor behavior is not my fault. Blame is the tool behind everyone who sees herself as a victim.

A victim carries the idea that there is no way to overcome or achieve anything. I am a result of the things done to me. When our identity is found in our victim-ness, we see our circumstances as chains that keep us from moving into anything of worth or value. When this is our state of mind, we have an intimate, albeit twisted, relationship with ourselves and our perpetrator. Blame and its partner, unforgiveness, are the shackles that do not allow our heart the ability to love and be loved by the One who knows us best: God.

Nearly knocking me over in her haste to tell me her story, Sarah approached me wild-eyed, perspiration beading on her upper lip, and her breath catching in her throat.

"That teacher on the platform has no idea what she is talking about and for that matter, is offensive to people like me," poking me in the shoulder to emphasize her point.

I did notice that this woman would be what some consider slightly overweight but did not put two and two together at first.

"She has NO IDEA what it's like to be me. I am a type 2 diabetic and I will never be better. My son has passed away and it was all the doctor's fault."

I was not tracking with this woman, who obviously was in great distress.

With as much grace and quickness I could gather I said, "I am so sorry. I am sure the speaker in her talk about how nutrition affects our whole life was not condemning you, but encouraging all of us to seek out a healthier lifestyle."

I was the Women's Ministry Director at our large church, and was asked by my senior pastor to have a 4-week study with an international speaker, so she could use our group as a way to film with an audience for her new bible study series she was producing.

I was quick to say yes to his offer. This was such a great way to engage women in our community of faith. This speaker had a way to connect with women I valued as she pointed them to Jesus in her teaching. As the event coordinator, I made sure there were enough volunteers to help with set-up, tear down and anything else this speaker would need. We had a great turn out and many women I had never seen before showed up.

The speaker had slightly touched on the fact that we are made up of body, soul and spirit and made mention that our nutrition can and will directly affect our soul. A healthy physical lifestyle was indeed a part of a healthy spiritual life. Five minutes into the 45-minute talk, was when I was approached by this hurt and angry woman. I realized quickly (maybe not a quickly as I could have) she was crying out for help. I shifted gears from defending our speaker to truly wanting to hear this woman's heart.

"I am so sorry it must be so painful as a mom to have lost your son. What was his name and how old was he?"

Stopping mid-breath, she said, "His name was John and he was 14 years-old. It was all the doctor's fault. They took my son."

As she went on, she got more angry. Her hurt quickly turned into bitterness and it was obvious that she was blaming every negative thing in her life to this one horrendous incident. My heart broke for her, to see how she was so deeply hurt and could only see everything through the lens of her son's death.

Her answer to my next question floored me. If I was off balance before it all but sat me on my rear. I asked, "When did he die?" I quietly asked her, and it took a few seconds for her to catch her breath.

"15 years ago," she gasped through strangled breath.

My initial thought was, "Oh, my goodness. I told her I was sorry for her loss. She walked away that night still angry, still bitter and even more convinced that the speaker had it out for her personally.

15 years is a long time to hold onto something. I am not saying that losing a child is not life altering, traumatic and horrendous, this is every mom's worst nightmare. In the pain of her son's death, all she could do was blame others and allow the tentacles of unforgiveness to tighten around her heart and dictate her every move. Being a victim is a lot of work. When we continue to play the blame game and hold onto the things that have been done to us or to the ones we love, we continue the cycle of hurt, anger and bitterness. Wearing a victim's clothing is like choosing to wear a T-shirt that's been rolled in poop and not expecting anyone to notice the smell and the stains. Wearing victimhood is stinky and off-. This behavior keeps us from relationships with others, and most importantly, the relationship with Jesus which will heal our hurts and clean up our mess.

Unforgiveness and blame are two of the biggest barriers to an intimate relationship with the One who adores us. These barriers stop us from crossing the threshold of a deep friendship and understanding with our Creator. We think and/or feel he is too far away or too unapproachable for us to connect. There is a sense of a wall between Him and us. A wall that we have constructed and God wants to tear down brick by brick.

Because we have built the wall, we are the ones who must find the tools to tear it down alongside God. A victim's wall may go up overnight or more likely be built brick by circumstantial brick. The base of the wall might be a cruel remark or unfair judgment followed by a broken trust and a lie about ourselves we believed.

How do we tear down the wall of victimness we mistakenly believe is protecting us? What can we do? Much like the Berlin Wall, that was reportedly built in 24 hours and took years to tear down, we must go through a process. Can you imagine what it must have been like for that very first person to walk across the border with soldiers standing guard? He must have been incredibly nervous. The day before his behavior would have warranted being shot in the back as he tried to escape, so it is with us as we quit the blame, shame game and lay down our right to be wronged.

The first step, as redundant as it sounds, is to quit blaming others for our circumstances. We start by allowing God to control our truth.

We can demolish every deceptive fantasy[a] that opposes God and break through every arrogant attitude that is raised up in defiance of the true knowledge of God. We capture, like prisoners of war, every thought[b] and insist that it bow in obedience to the Anointed One (2nd Corinthians 10:5 TPT).

The next thing we get to do is walk in forgiveness for ourselves and towards the ones who have wronged us. We will talk more about the process of forgiveness, what forgiveness is, and is not, later. The main thing to know about forgiveness, is not saying what was done to you was okay or did not happen. Your story is what defines you and to take away any part of it leads to more hiding.

The third tool to remove bricks in the wall is taking a step of involvement in a genuine and healthy community. You need a place where it is safe to trust others, a place where the language of grace is spoken and lived out. You need a place where grace is received and given, and the truth can be spoken. We were designed for relationship(s). It all started in the garden, remember?

Healthy community is essential in learning to believe what God says about us. Grace must be extended so we can learn to trust and to hear

God's truth about us. This is one of the risks we must take even though it may feel as if there is a "proverbial" gun to our back. Learning to be loved is the greatest part of our journey to freedom and intimacy.

As you relearn to trust God first, next we can learn to trust people in a healthy, lifegiving way. From the beginning, we were created to live in community with God and others. The enemy of our soul has been hard at work to interfere every step of the way. The thing is, the enemy cannot win unless we allow him.

His heart for you, as his ART, is to walk in intimacy and freedom.

ASK: God to show you an area in your life, where forgiveness needs to be applied either towards yourself or another person.

_____

_____

READ: *Forgive us the wrongs we have done as we ourselves release forgiveness to those who have wronged us* (Matthew 6:12 TPT).

The footnote in The Passion Translation for verse 12, "Send away the results of our debts (shortcomings)," used as a metaphor for our sins. The Aramaic can be translated, "Give us serenity as we also allow others serenity."

TELL: someone you trust about your choice to forgive and why.

PART TWO

Know
The Masterpiece

CHAPTER 4

What Medium Did the Master Use?

"You were designed to make a difference."

—Pastor Rick Warren

There she was. I had been waiting years to actually see her in person. My stomach was in knots and I was having a hard time containing my excitement. I had trounced through the whole museum for hours, trying my best to appreciate the statues from ancient Greece and the paintings from the early Baroque Era. I had taken one summer class on art history and knew I was NO expert, but there was one painting that I could not wait to see.

I entered a large dark room with several other large paintings, but as I gazed to my right, I saw a large crowd standing behind silk ropes with armed guards on either side. I made my way towards the crowd, trying my best to shoulder my way closer. My ears were assaulted by multiple languages, but it was clear everyone was excited to see what I so longed to catch a glimpse of. I pulled myself up to my full 5'4", to peek over the shoulder of the tourist in front of me. As I took in the full view, my heart went from a rapid burst to falling to my feet.

"Really, really that's it," I muttered, more to myself, than to my traveling companions.

La Gioconda's mischievous smile taunted me. The Mona Lisa, as she is known in English, in all her glory measured approximately 18"x32". In my mind, she was huge and almost mural like in size. But there she was, probably one of the most iconic paintings of our time and she was downright puny. In my mind, she had been built up so large that it was hard to fathom this priceless work of art was so ordinary in so many ways.

The Louvre, where she resides, gets 6 million visitors a year. It is estimated that 16,000 people crowd into the Salle des Etats (where she was housed) every day to gape at her.

She was stolen back in 1911, where she lay hidden under a bed in Italy for two years, and she has traveled all over the world. She is now housed in a special new $3.6 million room designed by a Peruvian architect.

She is an undisputed masterpiece of Leonardo Da Vinci. There is so much mystery surrounding her. A myriad of novels, sonnets and even movies have been written and produced about her. She is the subject of conspiracy theories and romantic rendezvous. Who she was, is up for discussion but who she is, is not. She is 'the masterpiece' of an amazing master. He lovingly painted her and designed her.

What makes her so unique was not so much the topic of the painting, but the artist that spent hours on her.

I doubt that she argued with Da Vinci, while she sat for him about which medium to use.

"Leo darling, I would be much better suited to be painted as a watercolor."

No, I am pretty sure she sat and was, for the *most* part, quiet - after all she was a woman.

The bible calls us His masterpieces, by the very nature the Master creator saw fit to create you. My hope as you turn the pages of this book and listen to voice of the one who created you through stories and self-examination you will come to see yourself as His masterpiece. You are so much more valuable than a painting that sits in a room for people to merely look at. You are a living, breathing, difference making, masterpiece.

We are all created using the same raw materials of DNA strands and molecules. These elements make up our organs, skin, \ bones, \hair color (even those of us who have had a little help from Miss Clairol) and the color of our eyes. All the same raw material is used, with a completely different result when combined in a unique way.

I am astounded even an identical twins have a different fingerprint or retina make-up. But what is most interesting to me is the fact our very personality is solely ours. Now there are similarities, much like a Monet watercolor may look a bit like a Van Gogh watercolor; however, even though each artist used the same medium they had two very different results.

You formed my innermost being, shaping my delicate inside and my intricate outside, and wove them all together in my mother's womb. I thank you, God, for making me so mysteriously complex! (Psalm 139:13-14 TPT)

He used the same raw materials and yet not one of us is like another in our physical appearance, our emotions and our personality or the gifts God has given us. We get the joy of uncovering and discovering who and what we are made of and why.

You do you!

Such a great saying, but really what does it mean? "You do you" and to heck with everyone else, what they think, or you be the only you there is and make the world a better place? We are going to go with the latter and look at your unique personality and how that can be used to make a difference in the world. There are about as many ways to describe personality as there are personalities. I am not going to define the difference between temperament and personality. I am not a psychologist nor a learned professor in the discipline. However, I will share one of the ways that made sense to me as I understood who I was made to be, and why my personality was such an important part of that story.

I had the joy and pleasure of studying under a woman by the name of Florence Littauer who along with her husband Fred, broke down the personalities in an easy-to-remember and easy-to-use fashion in many of their books. I am not going to do an exhaustive study, but I encourage you to read more for yourselves *

Let me invite you to a little party. You have arrived a bit early, due to the fact that traffic was not quite as bad as you had planned. Rather than sit in your car, you go ahead knock on the door and are welcomed in by the host. Walking into the large room you can't help but notice a woman who is in the middle of the room. She is standing with her hands on her hips and is loud (like outside voice loud.) She is telling others how to finish party prep and directing the caterer on where to place the food. There is no doubt she oversees this party, even though it is not at her house. Her calm assertiveness is meant to be listened to and obeyed.

You have just encountered our Powerful Choleric. Their motto in life is, "Let's do things the RIGHT way I.E. my way."

This personality is the natural born leader. They are goal oriented, results based, and in charge type of people. Their ability to delegate comes naturally and people follow their instructions. They can be bossy and overbearing, if not careful. They are the ones who will crusade for a cause and bring others along the journey. They are usually right about things, but often due to their perceived arrogance can be rejected by others.

The next person you notice is a handsome man dressed in neon green shorts with matching neon striped socks. He is surrounded by at least five others who were supposed to be there to help party setup, but they are obviously too enthralled in whatever the neon wearing man is talking about. Upon closer inspection, you can tell the man is telling a story about his latest trip to Disney World in which he was asked to join their creative team and make the next Pixar film. He too, is loud, much like our powerful choleric gal. He is using his hands to tell the story. You are a bit worried that if anyone gets too close, they might get whacked upside the head with his flying appendages. Everyone surrounding him is laughing and having a great time.

You have just been engulfed by our Popular Sanguine. Their motto is, "Let's do things the FUN way."

This personality is all about fun. They are open and spontaneous, which can make them suffer from foot in mouth disease. They love to be the center of attention and are great storytellers, if not always accurate, the story will be entertaining and fun. They do not know a stranger and they often will say the more the merrier, when it comes to including people. They bring laughter and positivity to most every situation they find themselves in. They bring out the best in people and believe in the innate goodness of everyone. They are a motivator, a promoter and can sell just about anything to anyone when they believe in something.

The next person you notice is the hostess that let you into the house. In fact, you realize that it is her home you are at. She is impeccably dressed and even though the invitation said casual dress, she is just a bit more dressed up than the rest. She has on jeans, which upon second glance you notice have a crease down the front because she has obviously ironed them. A crisp white shirt tucked into her jeans completes her ensemble. You notice that she has been following the people, finishing the setup and she's straightening up behind them. She has carefully rearranged the plates of food as they have been set on the table and double checked the list on her phone. She marks items as done, when she is satisfied with the result.

You have just met our Perfect Melancholy. Her motto is, "Let's do it the PERFECT way."

People with this personality type are probably the hardest on themselves because they desire perfection in an imperfect world. They believe perfection should be everyone's goal. They are extremely organized and creative. They love order and are deep thinkers. They would rather have one or two deep friendships which lovingly develop over time. The perfect melancholy is what some may call the classic introvert. This individual needs alone time to recharge, but is very thoughtful and always concerned about the feelings of others. The fact they expect perfection of others and even more perfection from themselves is why they tend to battle depression. These individuals need to bring order out of chaos and creativity out of nothing. Many of our artists are our melancholy friends.

The last person you notice is a man who is leaning against a wall and you can't help but wonder if he is wearing the clothes, he slept in. They are a pair of sweatpants and a T-shirt resembling workout clothes. You can tell from his stature and structure that he has not worked out in a while. You approach just close enough to hear him and the person he is talking to or should I say the person he is listening to. The person is telling him about the challenges he has faced at work this week and how hard it has been the last few years in his personal relationships. Our sweatpants wearing friend invites the other man to sit down on a nearby couch. He is very attentive in his listening and offers to pray with the other man right then and there.

You have just witnessed the Peaceful Phlegmatic in action. His motto is, "Let's do it the EASY way."

Peaceful Phlegmatics are easy going, peace loving and loved by pretty much everyone. They are the glue in many relationships because they have the ability to see an issue from all sides. They bring calm and comfort to most any situation. Their sense of humor is dry and laced with sarcasm, but seldom if ever, are they insensitive in their humor. They are kind, considerate and loyal. They do not get their feathers ruffled and as a result it can appear, they aren't motivated. They are slow to make decisions but once their mind is made up, they are immovable. They are considered to be the most stubborn of all of the personalities. They are needed to bring peace and tranquility to any situation and their diplomacy can help put out relational fires with ease.

These are broad generalizations, and no one is 100% any one personality. In fact, usually we are a combination of at least two. Taking time to understand how you are wired is the first step understanding why you see things that others may not see.

I believe we all carry some of the personality of God. As a result, with the Holy Spirits, we can use our God given personality to bring hope and help to this world. Like the artist that may create with marble, watercolor, oil paint or bronze God has designed you with a specific medium embodied by your personality.

There is an assessment at the end of the book, if you desire to look at the personalities more in depth. The idea is not to put any one in a box, yet rather let you out of the box to truly "do you!"

Do you as His ART!

ASK: yourself, which of the personalities do you see as your God given one? (If unsure, take the assessment in the back of the book.)

READ: *For we are God's masterpiece. He has created us anew in Christ Jesus, so we can do the good things he planned for us long ago.* (Ephesians 2:10 NLT)

TELL: God what your favorite part of your personality is.

*Take time to take the personality plus assessment at the back of the book. Appendix 1 and 2.

CHAPTER 5

Purpose in the Pain

Our Experiences Are the Chisel to Bring Out His beauty

"We do not suffer by accident"

–Jane Austen

C.S. Lewis in "The Problem of Pain" says, "We can ignore even pleasure. But pain insists upon being attended to. God whispers to us in our pleasures, speaks in our conscience, but shouts in our pains: it is his megaphone to rouse a deaf world." Pain is the human condition that causes change and how we deal with the painful experience is how we are changed. We can shake our fist at God and say, "Why me?" Or we can surrender to the love of Jesus and say, "Why not me?"

The fear crept in like a summer fog in the mountains, deceptively light and innocent. By the time I realized what had happened, I was paralyzed in fear and could not see my way out. I lay on my bed that night, shaking in fear as I was convinced that my marriage was ending, and my husband of almost 20 years was certainly going to abandon me and our four children. He was late again, out "working" and entertaining clients. He was not answering his phone and I was desperate to hear his voice.

This was not unusual. He worked many late nights. What made tonight so different was my response. That morning, my husband kissed me goodbye, reminding me of his late-night event and told me we would go on a date later in the week. The fog of fear did not happen overnight, even though it felt that way. The thoughts had come and gone quite a bit over the last few months, as my husband's schedule got busier. At first, it was easy to dismiss the thoughts that flitted their way through my heart. Silly things like, *"He almost forgot to kiss you this morning, don't you know that means he really doesn't care?"*

Or, *"What, no thanks for the dinner you slaved over. He just really doesn't appreciate all you do for him."*

You get the picture. They were somewhat innocuous and easily dismissed. But as those thoughts took root and became beliefs, my heart was in a million pieces and I in a panic trying to figure out how to take care of our four kids without my husband.

That night, I could no longer deny that I was in trouble. I had to lean into the one whom I knew had the answer, JESUS. I wish I could say that night I prayed, and all my care and concerns washed away. But there were many other nights that followed in which I battled my thoughts because that was exactly ALL they were- thoughts. None of it was true, my husband loved me, he would even say he adored me. He may have been a bit more distracted during this time. He was trying his best to provide for our growing family in a tough economy. The extra hours of work were not an escape plan from our family and marriage.

My uncaptured thoughts had gotten the best of me. My thoughts had turned into emotions, which consumed everything. I begged God to remove them, to help me stop them, and to be a better Christian by believing what God said about taking my thoughts captive. No amount of begging seemed to work. One night, again alone, as my husband worked late, I heard the voice of the one who loved me most. He said, "Rather than beg me to take them away, why don't you ask me why you have these thoughts?"

It never occurred to me that the thoughts were the ridiculous imaginings of a lonely housewife. That night, I did just that. I asked God to show me the root of the fear of being abandoned. Where did the seeds of doubt and fear come from?

I had an amazing childhood. My parent's marriage was referenced in marriage books on what a healthy marriage looked like. I had a secure home with parents who loved me and adored each other. The experts would say I should be the most secure of children who would grow up to be a secure adult. So, where in the heck had this anxiety and fear come from?

God reminded me of the night, when in the midst of a healthy and safe family I found myself as an 11-year old little girl in an unsafe place. I was with the wrong person at the wrong time. I had brushed this one-time occurrence under the carpet of lost memories. I hoped it really wasn't real that it would be truly forgotten. That experience, whether I realized it or not had impacted my heart and soul.

God showed me this was where the seed of doubt and fear had been unwittingly planted. It was dormant for many years, until my current circumstances watered that seed and the fear of abandonment grew into a full-grown plant. Because of my healthy family, my love of Jesus and being involved with some amazing women, with whom I felt somewhat safe with, I was able to share my experience. Their wise counsel and love began the turn around.

The healing process quickly turned my heart around towards my husband, and it helped me look at myself deeper. I began questioning some of the choices I made through the years.

The desperate need for acceptance, which allowed my beliefs to be compromised and the people pleasing to become unhealthily out of control. To choose people's approval, over what I knew in my heart was right. I was forced to look at those choices and experiences with a new lens. I could see the things done to me, whether by my choice or by the choice of others would no longer have a negative hold on me.

My journey into wholeness began, and a new hunger to see others set free from the same bondage I had experienced. Bondage from circumstances and lies spoken over them. The lies that cripple hope, and self-love, and feelings of unworthiness, even though there is a God who is crazy in love with them.

I did more research and discovered that 3 out of 4 women have had some kind of abuse in their life, and as a result felt unloved and unworthy. I made a conscious decision to not waste the experience that would or could be described as painful in my life. I wanted to be a difference maker in whomever God brought into my world.

I knew my story, needed to be shared and how God triumphed in my life. I knew my story of walking in forgiveness, towards my perpetrator, and for myself was key to helping others experience the love that Jesus has for them.

I know in my heart of hearts; God was right there in the pain and hurt. He did not cause the pain; He gave me the choice of what to do about it. He allowed me to say yes to His love and no to hurt, pain, and rejection that so easily could have been my identity.

Painful experiences are a part of living in a world that has walked away from its Creator. What we do with them is our responsibility, but we do not do this on our own. We have the promise of our helper, the Holy Spirit, who longs to see us walk in freedom. When we surrender our pain to the Holy Spirit, he can take it and remake it into something beautiful.

"And I will ask the Father and he will give you another Savior, the Holy Spirit of Truth, who will be to you a friend just like me—and he will never

leave you. The world won't receive him because they can't see him or know him.
But you will know him intimately, because he will make his home in you and
will live inside you" (John 14:16-17).

Jesus knew His purpose before he left heaven and stepped down to
earth. Simply put, He was to be the Savior of the world. Practically put,
He knew He was going to the cross to die a slow painful death so that we
would not have to. His purpose was not all waterfalls and butterflies, yet he
went willingly.

Her smile was the first thing that I noticed; the next thing was her
elegant presence. She was a beautiful woman and when she introduced
herself, her sweet melodic Hispanic accent was ever so slight.

"Hi, my name is Anel. I am so excited to meet you and start studying
the bible in evening college."

Our church had recently merged with a fabulous Spanish language
congregation. Now you need to know, that I believe Jesus is part Latino
because He demonstrates the Latin heart and joy of living that some of us
Anglos are a little less demonstrative about. I was overjoyed that we were
starting this new journey with our brothers and sisters who were so much a
part of living in the southwest. I had met Anel That first night of the bible
college I oversaw at our church.

Anel was one of the precious members who was now a part of our
church family. I got to know Anel first, through her ever-present serving.
It did not matter what we asked her to do her answer was always a
resounding yes.

As I got to know Anel more, I heard her story, she was a 14-year breast
cancer survivor due to the illness and/or treatments she had sustained heart
damage and was fit with a pacemaker. She was a young woman in her
early 40s, but this did not define her and in fact you seldom if ever heard
about it.

She served in every capacity. One of her greatest gifts to us, was her
Spanish language translation services. She understood how important
it was. Her influence was wide-reaching. Oftentimes, she often brought
women to me who needed a little bit of encouragement or prayer. She was a
fierce warrior for women and children.

About four years into our friendship the cancer came back with a vengeance and she started treatments again. She would have as many as five rounds of chemo one right after another while pursuing alternative medical options. This did not seem to slow her down. In fact, I think it fired her up.

I believe it was during this time that her sense of purpose was heightened. She became even more vigilant concerning injustice and helped bring to light a serious situation regarding one of our youth - even though she was in the middle of fighting for her life.

Anel was a woman on a mission, and as she continued her treatments she never wavered. There came a point, where the treatments no longer were making any headway and she made the decision to stop treatments. Which seemed to only solidify her purpose more. Everyone she came in contact with heard about her Jesus. She made sure not one opportunity was missed.

I had the honor and extreme privilege of officiating Anel's celebration of life when she passed from the earth to her home in heaven. Story after story was told about Anel's impact and how she led so many to Jesus. In fact, her aunt, the day after Anel went to be with the Lord, shared a story with Anel's friends. "I want what she had; I want what you have."

That day her aunt made a commitment to follow Jesus.

During her celebration of life service, an observation was made that she had battled cancer for 17 years in one way or another. And maybe, just maybe, she had held on that long because she wanted as many people as possible know her Jesus in the intimate way, she knew Him. Her joy, strength, peace and hope were contagious, and it was these qualities that attracted so many to her. Always her answer to them was "It's all about Jesus."

"Purpose, when directed heavenward helps us rise above the circumstances and allows us to use the circumstance to define our purpose and to live it out."
Ruth Mitchell

ASK: Has there been a time when circumstances seemed so overwhelming or painful, and you were not sure how it was going to work out? Can you see God's hand during that time? If not, take time to ask God for his perspective on the situation.

_____

_____

READ: John 14:16-17 *And I will ask the Father and he will give you another[a] Savior,[b] the Holy Spirit of Truth, who will be to you a friend just like me—and he will never leave you. The world won't receive him because they can't see him or know him. But you will know him intimately, because he will make his home in you and will live inside you.*

TELL: someone about a painful experience you have had and how it has shaped you into a better person.

CHAPTER 6

How Has the Master Molded Your Heart?

"God has to break you deeply before he can use you greatly"

—A.W. Tozer

Hot wet tears burned my cheeks as they ran down my face.

"How could you do this to me?"

"You made a mistake and called the wrong girl."

I had begged God and my missions pastor, not necessarily in that order, to take me to Africa. Now that I was here, I knew it was the biggest mistake I had ever made. I had seen things I could never un-see. Worse I had smelled things I could never un-smell.

Poverty has a smell , I have long since smelled and learned to recognize. It is a mixture of burning garbage, raw sewage and despair, a smell which burns your eyes and heart, and almost always results in tears. This smell robs everyone of any hope for tomorrow or even for today.

After returning from a walking tour of the largest slum in Nairobi, Kenya, my heart was shattered into a million pieces. Astoundingly, it was something I asked God for. I had prayed the dangerous prayer of, "God break my heart for what breaks yours."

I was distraught and felt helpless as I lay face down on my pillow that night in Nairobi. I tried my best not to disturb my roommate with my tears, that threatened to turn into sobs. What did God think he was doing by bringing this middle-aged, middle class and extremely white American women to Africa.

That day we visited the Kibera slum. Kibera is the largest slum in Nairobi, and the largest urban slum in Africa. The population is estimated anywhere between 200,000 and 1 million. The living conditions of which I would not want my enemy's' cat to live in. That day we were walking with an energetic and military-like woman, who was determined to be a difference maker in the slum. She showed us ways to get involved as a church. We saw various organizations making a small dent in the overwhelming problem that faced those living within the boundaries of Kibera.

I thought I was coming to "make a difference." There was no way! With a broken heart and no way to get home, I laid on my bed feeling overwhelmed and over emotional. No way home and all I wanted to do, that night, was run away. I wanted to run back to my comfortable way of thinking, run back to my nice home, run back to my nice coffee shop and my nice mall! I wanted to take back the dangerous prayer I had prayed.

That night, the gentle voice of my Lord said, "Do you trust me?" He whispered in my ear, "Are you now ready to listen to me?"

"What choice do I have? "I replied to my Jesus.

I had come to know His voice above my own emotions. I knew I could trust that voice.

"I know how your heart breaks and I am aware of each individual that is suffering and yes my heart too, is broken. But it is not broken beyond repair. Trust me and learn to listen to my voice for direction," He said.

The next day after a fitful night's sleep, we traveled outside of the city center to another place of outreach. As we traveled, my companions chattered amongst themselves. I was still in deep thought and prayer. He again whispered in my heart, "Trust me."

We pulled into a small church building that was used as a meeting place for a group of women, who all were either infected or affected by HIV. These beautiful women gathered weekly to share and pray for one another. After a time of the women formally sharing what the purpose of the ministry was, the rest of my group went on a tour of the church and facilities. I opted to stay outside and stand in the African dust and chat with these women.

I wanted to know each of them and hear their story. Knowing time was limited, we did quick introductions and as it turned out two of the women were named Ruth. Laughter burst from their beautiful mouths, as I joked about all of the Ruth's looking like one another.

A strong sense came into my heart. "Ruth, I want you to share with these women my heart." I cautiously asked, "Would you like to hear my favorite verse and how I see you all are walking this out through your ministry to one another?"

"Oh yes," my new friends responded.

"For you are God's masterpiece created in Christ to do good work which he prepared beforehand so that we would walk in them" (Ephesians 2:10).

A few blank stares made it evident they could not exactly understand what I had just said. Again, in my heart I heard the voice of my Savior.

"They do not know what a masterpiece is. Use a different word."

The word that immediately came to my mind just felt contrived and overused.

"God not that word."

I continued to argue for a few moments with God, and anyone knows that when you argue with God, you will always lose.

"That means you are all *special*, there is no one else like you." I said this in a voice that was a bit shakier than I had planned.

"SPECIAL," they all nodded in unison.

A few pieces of my heart were mended that day as I realized I never was meant to be the one to change the world, rescue the poor or be any kind of white horse-riding hero. That was Jesus' job. My job was to listen to Him and share His heart through words and deeds. At that moment, I heard God's voice from His place of a broken heart for humanity.

"People matter to God and they need to know that."

In the middle of that trip, all I wanted to do was run from the pain and all God wanted me to do was to run to His arms and bring the pain to Him to rework and reframe it for His good.

God wanted my heart broken so He could rebuild it. So, my God born passion could move from emotion to action. That is always God's plan. He wants to use our brokenness to put action to our purpose, if we will let him.

Kathy was a beautiful petite blonde with big dreams and plans in her heart. With hopes high she married her college sweetheart. They were in Bible college together with plans of going on the mission field upon graduation. Her husband earned his pilot's license so they could fly medical missions. As her husband focused on his piloting skills, his mission dreams faded from his heart. In less than five years into the marriage, her husband came to her and declared not only did he no longer want to be a missionary, he also no longer believed in God! Her heart was smashed into a million pieces.

I met Kathy about the time this devastating revelation took place. We began what we called our "praying wives club" with another one of our friends. We would spend hours upon hours every Tuesday morning, consuming too much coffee, praying and believing for our husbands and families.

Kathy upon discovering her husband's inability to remain faithful to his wedding vows, and his unwillingness to change, faced the hardest decision of her life. She and her husband dissolved their marriage. It was the end of her dream and her heart was shattered again.

I watched as she slowly pulled her life back together. In the midst of her pain she made a decision that changed the trajectory of her life. She went back to school to become a counselor, to speak life into women and men who faced heartache and pain.

20 years later, she has a thriving practice and on a daily basis makes a huge difference in many people's lives. Her brokenness surrendered to a loving God was used to propel her into her passion and purpose. Her mission field is not on foreign soil, but right in her backyard. She has reached people she never could have if she had not allowed the master sculptor to work on her heart.

Passion is almost always born out of pain. It may be your own personal pain or pain of others. This is a powerful tool to propel us into what God has planned for us. I am not saying that God caused the pain, but He definitely will use it if we allow Him.

What broken your heart? What brings you to tears or to righteous indignation?

These answers can and will reveal the passion that God has placed in your heart.

"Passion without the particulars is just an emotion" Pam Farrel.

In my life, I have met many passionate people. They are full of righteous anger at the injustices in the world and can pontificate all day long about how things should and could be different. I have also met some folks who with very few words are changing the world we live in. Passion without a plan is simply a feeling.

Because we carry God's DNA, we carry his heartbeat for humanity within us. The way we discover that heartbeat is simple, but profound. Simply put, we spend time with our master creator. We give him full access to mold and shape our heart, like a sculptor with a bit of clay (Jeremiah 18:6). As the clay is in the potter's hand, so are you in my hand.

The potter's constant pressure in our lives molds us into what His plan is for us. That pressure comes in various ways. Though, most often, it's through heartache and pain as we realize our dependency on God for everything. The pressure can be a light touch as we press into Him and learn what His heart breaks for, what His heart beats for.

Something strange and wonderful happens when we spend time with the one who loves us most. Science has proven lover's hearts beat with the same rhythm. If you hooked them up to an echocardiogram the rhythm on the tape out-put would look similar. The one we spend the most intimate time with physically shapes the inner world of our heartbeat. As we spend time with the lover of our soul, our heart begins to align with and beat in the same rhythm as our Creator's. What breaks His heart will break ours. His passion will become our passion.

As we allow the Master Creator to mold us, mend us and as we spend time getting to know His heart, we become the beautiful sculpture He can use and display His passion through.

ART

Digging into what you are passionate about is not just an exercise in emotional weightlifting. The reason you need to identify what you are passionate about is so you can understand the framework God has used to mold your heart. Take some time to look at his ART.

A SK:

- What makes you come alive?
- What will you do, when you've found your passion?
- What would you be willing to try again, even after a failure?
- Is there a common theme with the verses in the Bible that you have underlined or highlighted?
- What's been a common theme in your life? What's something that people would say about you, in each job you've held?
- What skills come to you naturally? How could you possibly use those to make a living? (Get creative, this is just a brainstorming activity.)
- What types of things do friends, colleagues, and/or family usually seek your input for?
- What would you do for nothing? If you didn't have to worry about money, what would you be doing? (Again, this is just hypothetical.)
- What's something that, when immersed in it, you lose track of time?
- What gets your blood boiling? What's a problem in the world that you'd love to fix?

R EAD: *He said, "Can I not do with you, Israel, as this potter does?" declares the Lord. "Like clay in the hand of the potter, so are you in my hand, Israel."* Jeremiah 18:6. *But who are you, a human being, to talk back to God? "Shall what is formed say to the one who formed it, 'Why did you make me like this?'"* Romans 9:20.

T ELL: someone what you think your God-sculpted passion is and why?

CHAPTER 7

Waiting for the Paint to Dry

Purpose In The Waiting

"I created a vision of David in my mind and simply carved away everything that was not David."

–Michelangelo

Michelangelo created *David* from a piece of marble that had been twice discarded by other sculptors. Agostino di Duccio gave up on a project using the block, it sat untouched for 10 years. Antonio Rossellino took the next crack at the block but decided it was too much of a pain to work with. When Michelangelo finally got his hands on it, the marble had been waiting for 40 years for someone who was up to its challenge.

If you find your season as one sitting in the back of the marble yard, waiting for the master to release you into your "purpose," to quote my dad, "don't sweat it." This is much easier for me to say, than for me to live out. When we begin to realize we have a unique calling or purpose, if you are anything like me, you will be ready to take hell on with your super soaker. How come no one is crashing down my door and asking me to come and save the day.

What should I do in the waiting?

"And this is no empty hope, for God himself is the one who has prepared us for this wonderful destiny. And to confirm this promise, he has given us the Holy Spirit, like an engagement ring, as a promise" (2 Corinthians 5:5 TPT).

Through tears streaming down her sweet adolescent face, my daughter cried out her frustration. "Mom, why is my dream not good enough for my school counselor? When I told her what I wanted to be when I grew up, she told me that was not good enough. You know all I have ever really wanted was to be a mom." She was 13 or 14 at the time, and my response rolled easily off my tongue. "Baby, God knows your heart and He will make you a mom when the time is right."

Fast forward as I watched my little girl, all grown up, walk down the aisle to marry her high school sweetheart. I knew this man was the one we had prayed for long before we even knew his name. They were about to begin their life as husband and wife. Shortly after getting married, they were called into ministry. They worked in a Christian children's home, a place for kids whose parents were not able to take care of them. A welcoming home for kids and place parents and grandparents could trust to help keep their children out of the foster system.

I watched as my daughter and her husband decided it was now time to begin a family of their own. Three months of trying turned into two years, and the doctors kept saying they were young and would have babies soon. Two years turned into five years.

My daughter and son-in-love watched as their friends, cousins and siblings began having babies. They moved to Ohio to be a part of a church, overseeing the children's ministry and the ministry to young adults. Still, no babies. tears over the phone, (this was pre-facetime) I would talk with, pray with and mostly cry with my girl as she waited for it to be her turn.

Later they discovered that there were some issues which more than likely would prevent them from conceiving. They decided adoption might be an answer and began to pray about it. During their stay in Ohio, one of the children from their first ministry job at the children's home called them out of nowhere. and told them she was pregnant at 15-years and she wanted them to have the baby.

They began the preparations with classes, finding an attorney and prepping for this gift coming their way. They found out she was having a girl and began to pray about names and how this gift would change their life. The weekly calls from momma became bi-weekly, then monthly and then no calls. Understandably, my kids grew concerned when phone calls from them to the biological mother were not returned.

Finally, they received a response. But it was the biological grandmother. She was never in favor of the adoption. She called to inform my kids that they had changed their mind and she was going to keep the baby and raise her. Another arrow of disappointment hit hard. They were back to waiting.

They returned home to Arizona to accept a job as youth pastors at the church they met and fell in love at in the high school group. This church was where my son-in-love first heard the call. It was on a mission trip to Argentina, when there was a prophesy over his life that he would be the father to many. This word of encouragement stayed with him and my daughter as they lived their ministry life.

As a church family, we decided that we would enter the crisis plaguing our state of over 16,000 children in foster care. Many of them lived in group homes or worse slept on the floors of our child welfare offices. As a church we knew the words of James 1:27. It discusses pure religion being involved with widows and orphans. Our modern orphan was the child in foster care, who was torn from the only family they may have known, and thrust into a place where they may or may not be loved. During this time my kids put their hands up to volunteer, and step into this world.

They went through classes, did all the prep work and were ready. When they got a call, that once again due to a clerical error, their fingerprint card was lost, and they had to wait. There they were, once again in the waiting room of purpose. When would it be their turn?

On a hot August morning the call came, there was a baby boy who needed a home. This tiny drug exposed baby came home with them and at first glance they were smitten. They were not sure if this precious little boy, who in the early days shook with the symptoms of opiate withdrawal and seldom slept for more than a couple hours at a time, would be in their home permanently. But they chose to love with total abandonment and not allow the past disappointments to define how they loved.

Jojo, as he has affectionately become known by, did go on to become their forever child through adoption and he is amazing. Through foster care and adoption God has brought two more boys into their family. Number three foster son, at the time of writing this book, is less than two weeks from being a part of our family - forever as their adopted son. With each child they have chosen to love with the abandon that God loves us with. The love is freely given with no expectation of return, but the return has been 100 times what they have given.

This is not the end of the story. My daughter still longed to carry a child of her own and give birth. The was what she had always felt was a part of her purpose. They took steps with the generosity of family, friends and an amazing doctor to pursue IVF. Their first attempt failed and we all went through the grieving process. When they were about to do another round of treatments, they got the call that the biological mom of their first born was expecting. They were asked if they would consider a kinship placement, until the mother was clean. Yes, was the quick answer. They put their plans on hold. This little one is their third son and is the one who will fully be theirs through adoption in a couple of weeks.

They decided to move forward with the next round of IVF. They are expecting not one, but two children. She is expecting a double blessing and so it appears this "childless couple" will be a family of seven soon. God's "no" has turned into a resounding "YES"! (By the way, please pray for me as the grandma of all these little ones. I am tired just thinking about it but my heart is overwhelmed with His love.)

Nine years of waiting in His waiting room thinking they were ready, but God's no was really a yes to something greater.

"God's "no" is actually a "yes" to something so much greater." —Josue Sanchez

But they who wait for the Lord shall renew their strength;
they shall mount up with wings like eagles;
they shall run and not be weary;
they shall walk and not faint. (Isaiah 40:31)

When we wait, we gain strength. This waiting in not a sitting back and taking a nap kind of wait. The meaning of the word wait means to trust with expectation of what God is going to do. The time when we feel as nothing is happening is when we turn and face our master with expectancy trusting growth is happening even when we may not see it.

If God had said yes to my kids, when they first started trying to get pregnant, where would those three little boys be? They have become our forever kids and grandkids. They have impacted not just my family's life, but the lives of so many who have come to know and love them.

God knows when the time is right. Our response during the waiting is our responsibility. In the waiting we may feel as if we are hidden, but in the hiddenness, we become strengthened, if we will trust God. How are you in the waiting? If you are like me, it varies from day-to-day.

I know God is trustworthy and will do what he has promised in my head, but my heart takes time to understand what waiting truly produces. He never stops working, even when we do not see it. He has given us the promise of His Holy Spirit to help us walk this out. Waiting feels like no movement at times, but God is never at a standstill.

How can we then wait well?

My kids waited well. They took what was in their hands at the time and lived as if the promise was already fulfilled. They said yes to parenting the children of others. They said yes to God and said no to feeling sorry for themselves.

They put their hope in God, not in what was the reality, of "no kids". The words hope and wait are found in Isaiah. This comes from the word in the Hebrew that means to be entwined much like a rope is twisted together for strength. This brings to mind the scripture found in Ecclesiastes, which talks about the 3-strand chord which is not easily broken. When we entwine ourselves with the Holy Spirit and the promise of God, our hope will not be broken, and we will gain strength in the waiting rather than becoming weary. Weariness comes when we constantly look at where we are and measure it up against where we want to be, or worse where others are.

Waiting well is about focusing on what God is doing in the quiet. Focusing on how we can continue to be entwined in God and not how others are doing. Not getting caught in the comparison trap.

Waiting well is active, not passive. Waiting is about honing our talents and giving of our treasures. My kids continued to study and to show themselves approved. This can be a time when we refine our craft or learn how to be better at what He has called us to. In the waiting, what are you doing? Are you taking courses to be better at what he has called you to? Are you volunteering in an area that stirs your heart for your passion? Are you helping someone else who is doing what you feel called to do?

Waiting well is about facing and overcoming discouragement, disappointment and disillusionment. Waiting is about growth or it might be God is still at work removing the unneeded piece of you that will take away from the masterpiece he sees below all of the your "hard" parts. The pieces of marble that are unnecessary and, in many ways, a hinderance to who you are.

Lord you know all my desires and deepest longings. My tears are liquid words and you can read them all. (Psalm 38:9 TPT)

ART

ASK: Have you been in a season of waiting? Or are you in the waiting room right now? What is the hardest part for you to trust God with?

READ: *But those who wait for the Lord [who expect, look for, and hope in Him] Will gain new strength and renew their power; They will lift up their wings [and rise up close to God] like eagles [rising toward the sun]; They will run and not become weary, They will walk and not grow tired.* Isaiah 40:31 (AMP).

TELL: God if you are in a season of waiting, you are choosing to trust Him. Or if your season of waiting is over tell, God how grateful you are for that time of hiddenness and growth.

PART THREE

Know the Master's Plan

CHAPTER 8

Unveiling The Masterpiece

"The great courageous act that we must all do, is to have the courage to step out of our history and past so that we can live our dreams."

–Oprah Winfrey

Here's another way to put it: You're here to be light, bringing out the God-colors into the world. God is not a secret to be kept. We're going public with this, as public as a city on a hill. If I make you light-bearers, you don't think I'm going to hide you under a bucket, do you? I'm putting you on a light stand. Now that I've put you there on a hilltop, on a light stand—shine! Keep open house; be generous with your lives. By opening up to others, you'll prompt people to open up with God, this generous Father in heaven. (Matthew 5:14 MSG).

I was wedged in the back seat, between my beautiful friend and her daughter. The driver was doing her best to avoid the potholes, as we traveled down the narrow streets and the car continued to bump along. Winding our way through unmarked streets, passing dilapidated homes and lean-to market fronts we arrived at our destination. The small, well kept, home was hidden behind walls and gates with razor wire to discourage intruders.

This was Cape Town and we were driving into the Elsies River township. A primarily colored neighborhood, the gorgeous group of mixed races included Indian, African and European. It was home to my friend's great aunt - the friend whose lap I almost was sitting on in the back seat of the sturdy little car.

The gate opened to reveal a sweet little yellow home with a white door. We were ushered in as if we were royalty. My friend embraced her aunt, as if it had been a lifetime since she had seen her, and in fact it had been several years. Beautiful sturdy brown arms embraced me just as tightly. I took a seat in the corner on a well-loved yellow upholstered chair. Knowing in my heart I was about to witness something few outside their family ever saw.

The excited voices of women, who had not seen each other in a long time filled the room. I did not understand a word they said, but I totally understood what they were saying. Between kisses and hugs, it was evident they were talking about the same things women talk about all over the world - their kids, husbands or lack thereof, the price of coffee and the latest neighborhood gossip.

The tone quickly grew serious as they passed the tea cookies and offered me a steaming hot cup of Rooibos tea from a cheery yellow patterned teapot. It did not take a genius to know the octogenarian who owned this home loved the color yellow. I felt so honored, as it was clear the treasured china cups and saucers were brought out only for special occasions.

The eldest woman, who was the matriarch of the family, soon began to dominate the conversation and as I leaned in my friend translated for me.

She said, "I have lived in this very neighborhood since the very beginning and though it was hard growing up here, we knew we were safe from each other. Lately it has become so hard to know who to trust. Just last week one of the teachers was shot, gangs have become rampant and kids are afraid to go to school. The schools are no longer a safe haven and we as the women in this area need to stand up for what is happening in our community. We have written letters to the magistrate but have not heard from him and it is time to no longer sit and wait to see what will happen."

The younger women in the room all nodded in agreement. I knew I was a part of something so special that afternoon, as they trusted me to hear about their fears and challenges as they began to problem solve. As the time grew short and we needed to leave, I watched as these women tearfully embraced each other and promised it would not be this long again before they gathered.

As we wedged ourselves back into the little car, my friend leaned over and whispered, "You are the only white woman who has ever been in my auntie's home."

Humbled to the very core of my being, I definitely shed more than a tear or two.

Pulling away my friend, in her quiet contemplation, slowly poured her heart out to me.

She said, "Ruthie, no one besides God will ever know their names outside of this small town and yet they are standing up for injustice. Their voices for the lost and the underdog will make a difference, I pray."

That afternoon again confirmed we need each other, and we all are created to make a difference. Hiding behind closed doors and hoping the world will change is not the answer. That afternoon tea with wise and justice minded women was proof to me that we are wired to make a difference, when we are tuned into *who* God says we are. The power of standing together and standing for one another as women is what the world needs!

We need to champion one another and believe the best of each other. Sitting in the corner, in what almost felt like eavesdropping, on a sacred moment showed me that we cannot hide away in our safe little world. We must stand up and speak up for what God has put in our hearts. These women were not worried about what they did not have and understood they held the answer for their community. They knew they had to be the light, and the ones to make change happen. Hiding was no longer an option.

Something happens when we allow God to break our hearts for what breaks His. We are faced with a choice. To simply feel bad and stay silent or be moved to action so the world may know the heart of our God for people. Each one of us, because we are made in His image, have a role to play. We each carry a God-ordained piece of the puzzle of God's heart. If we choose to hide that piece out of fear or worry, then the world is missing out.

"Won't you tell me, lover of my soul, where do you feed your flock? Where do you lead your beloved ones to rest in the heat of the day? For I wish to be wrapped all around you, as I go among the flocks of your under-shepherds. It is you I long form with no veil between us" (Song of Songs 1:7 TPT).

The lover in the Song of Songs had one desire: to be where her lover was at work. God's unfailing love for us draws us into a love relationship with Him. Our love filled heart's bent, is to desire to be where He is at work. When we follow Him to where He is at work it is only natural for us to join him doing that work. It then becomes our calling, desire and passion to make it known where he is working. To show the world through our actions how the one who loves us most, stands up for those who may not even know Him.

Matthew in the words of Jesus tells us like it is! Our purpose is to be the light on a hill. Not to cover and hide. Not to wait until we have it all together, which just in case you have not realized will not happen until you are seeing Jesus face-to-face in heaven. This is not optional, if we are to live a life of purpose and to fulfill our potential.

The unveiling of who we are in Jesus is the beginning of the process. Unlike a "masterpiece" that must wait for a public unveiling when it is complete and perfect, we have the joy of giving the world a view of what it looks like to be a work in process. The process is what the world needs to see. How God is shaping you, painting you and transforming you into the very image of the Master Artist.

The world needs to know that we come to God an unformed mess. He takes it and lovingly shapes us into His idea of what you can be. The transformation process is how we point people to Jesus. He sees and treats us as His masterpiece, even before the work is done. He pulls out our greatness as he shapes us. This is the greatness He gave us before we were even born.

As we give God permission to use our passions, gifts, personalities and experiences (good or bad) to sculpt us, the world, my friend, is watching. If we allow them the sneak peek of what it feels and looks like to be molded and loved, it will entice them to want the same thing. Allowing God to use our pain as a chisel to remove parts that we do not need, our gifts as paint on a brush, and our personality as refined on the potter's wheel, we allow the world to see it is ok to trust the master to make us into His image.

ART

ASK: What am I doing to show the world why God has broken my heart? How am I being a light on a hill?

_____

_____

READ/REFLECT: 14 "You are the light of the world. A town built on a hill cannot be hidden." (Matthew 5:14 *NIV*). How are you hiding?

TELL: someone what you believe God has called you to do and be, even if you are not sure yet.

CHAPTER 9

Never Too Late

What to Do When I Am No Longer in "Vogue"

"Aging is an extraordinary process where you become the person you always should have been."

—David Bowie

old and I am scared," the soft-spoken tender-hearted woman
in me. "I have been looking for a new job and I do not think I
much to offer."

I wish this was the first time I heard these words, but the truth is we are in such a youth obsessed society. Anyone older than 45 is now considered old, if we believe the media!

I reminded my new friend that one statistic says, we may be living to the ripe old age of 120 years - which meant she wasn't even halfway through her life. The truth is that none of us know when we will be seeing Jesus face-to-face, but until that time I believe we are not done growing and learning. The minute we stop learning is the time we should probably pack it up and sit in a rocking chair all day. All kidding aside, there is a real dilemma surrounding aging.

We live in a fast-paced world and it is changing faster than any time in our history. Before you turn your new mobile device on, there is a new and improved version and if you don't have it you and your device are obsolete. If you think I am kidding, just last month when I bought a new phone (my 18-month old grandson had thrown mine into our neighborhood lake) the tech savvy millennial genius was dumb founded when I told him I did not want the latest and greatest upgrade. I liked my phone, I liked that I did not have to ask my 10-year-old granddaughter to help me, which I would have to do if I bought a new one.

As amazing as it is to live during this time, we have created a mindset that says we are no longer in vogue if we have reached a certain age. Worse, many of us have allowed our own thoughts to convince us that we must put our dreams and aspirations on the shelf to gather dust as we slowly fade into the "sunset" of our lives.

Rather than sitting back and waiting during this time of our life, we have to be even more proactive to step into who and what God has called us to. This may look different and, in most cases, it will be necessary for us to adapt and change.

"The measure of intelligence is the ability to change."—Albert Einstein

"We are just trying to make sure that we make room for the next generation." Those are the words I have heard from many leaders lately.

Leaders in all sectors from business to church life have uttered those words. Countless articles and even books have been written on this topic. In theory those words sound great and are needed; however, when we take a deeper look, what does it say to those who are still in the productive time of their life, in other words those of us still breathing?

I am part of an amazing movement in the church and we are seeing the rise of gifted and called young adults. So, I do not want anyone to think I begrudge their place in this world. The problem occurs when we displace people, instead of helping them move on and up to the next phase of their own personal journey. We literally and figuratively push them out of the way. This results in a huge void and vacuum in the person's life - and dare I say in the life of the organization they were a part of.

If we believe in the value of human life, then why do we insist to those in the second half move over and out? Having experienced firsthand the sting of what it feels like, my heart cries out *"but I am not DONE yet"* and that is the truth. None of us are done until we see Jesus face-to-face. So then how do we truly link arms with one generation to the next, to accomplish all that God has called us to personally and most importantly He has called His Church to?

When I look at scripture, I see a clear pattern. Paul and Timothy. Elijah and Elisha. Elizabeth and Mary. Clearly it was relational. One did not exist without the other. There was what I see as an *"alongside"* ministry. The other thing I see is that the younger had a distinctly different call and did not take the "place of" the one who came before them, but with their unique gifts furthered the cause.

What is my responsibility as an "older"? It certainly is not to mandate or dictate what is best, but to model what I have learned. It is not about techniques or even styles but about heart and attitude. There are certain skills that certainly can be taught, but most everything else should be able to be caught.

I find myself at a crossroads in finding my place. For most of my ministry, I have been a doer /leader/ teacher. Follow me as I follow Jesus, that part will not change but the doing part must change. It is not time for me to "not do" but it is time for me to find out what I am "to be" about.

The areas of deficit I see in the next generation have so much to do with character development and the why behind the what. I grew up in what I would call the beginning of the "Christian celebrity." Where we saw the rise and fall of the TV evangelist which was documented on the nightly news. Celebrity was considered the pinnacle of success by many, but fame is fleeting. Charisma will not take you as far as character. Now with the internet and social media and reality TV, everyone can be famous.

I truly believe my job as a post 50 woman is to equip in character, calling and commitment the next generation and then commission them into what they are called to. How can this best be done, without "telling" the next generation what to do or think?

I must learn how to speak so people will listen, or more importantly act so people want to imitate. Millennials have gotten the worst wrap. Even though some of those generalities are true, I know some very hard working, eager to learn 20-somethings and at the same time I know some lazy, know it all 50-somethings.

So, if you find yourself saying, "But I am not done yet!" What is your responsibility? What are your next steps?

1. Acknowledge that it might be time to transition to the next thing.

I have been doing some of the same things for 27 years in ministry and I am more than ready, to not be "doing" them anymore. In fact, I am searching for the replacement for those things; however, I want to hand them off well.

2. Acknowledge that my way may not be the best way now.

Help those I hand off to understand HOW and WHY things were done a certain way but be open to conversations as to why that may no longer work. Allow them to experiment, fail, experiment and/or succeed.

3. Acknowledge the need for a relationship of trust with each other.

None of this works without trust being established. It is not an overnight accomplishment and many who are looking at us have had trust broken over and over again. They come from broken families, broken relationships and world of compromise.

"Trust is built and maintained by many small actions over time."

4. Acknowledge that I am ultimately responsible for what I leave behind.

When I look at what I will be known for, I hope and pray it is not about the tasks I accomplished, but for the lives that I touched and changed. If my identity is in my "doing" this is hard to comprehend, but if my identity is first in who Jesus says I am and second in who and how I have influenced, my task, title or accomplishment won't matter. I will continue to 'be" who I am no matter what.

So, what do I hope the generation following me will see and want to do?

1. Acknowledge that I may actually have something to teach you.

As one who has been where the 20-something sits, believe me when I understand what it felt like to think I knew more than the one who went before me. Once I took time to watch and listen to those who went before me, their stories, accomplishments and influences shaped my character, competence and commitment and the way I thought. I know I learned more by observing how things were done, than by reading books and or attending classes

2. Acknowledge and don't assume that my dreams have been fulfilled or my goals have been accomplished.

Though I have been running this race for longer than many 20-somethings have been alive, I am not tired! I have so much more that God has placed in my heart to accomplish and I do not want to accomplish it in a generational vacuum. I want to link arms with you and learn from you as you learn from me. And yes, I want to have a relationship with you.

3. Acknowledge just because I may not be current with ALL the trends, they are just that - trends and they will change.

This does not make me less knowledgeable, just not as trendy. Maybe take some time to let me know what is so important about those trends. Trends come and go, but relationships can and will last a lifetime.

4. Acknowledge my desire to finish well and be prepared to take the baton I am willing to hand over, when I see you have put in the heart work.

I know that you have been born into an Insta-society and it is amazing, colorful, fun and satisfying but sometimes those things we have to wait for are the sweetest in life.

Also remember the "classics" never go out of style.

Oprah Winfrey shared in an O Magazine feature, "We live in a youth-obsessed culture that is constantly trying to tell us that if we are not young, and we're not glowing, and we're not hot, that we don't matter. I refuse to let a system or a culture or a distorted view of reality tell me that I don't matter. I know that only by owning who and what you are can you start to step into the fullness of life. Every year should be teaching us all something valuable. Whether you get the lesson is really up to you."

ART

ASK: God what is it that you want me to do in this season of my ministry and life?

_____

_____

READ: *We've heard true stories from our fathers about our rich heritage. We will continue to tell our children and not hide from the rising generation the great marvels of our God—his miracles and power that have brought us all this far. The story of Israel is a lesson in God's ways. He established decrees for Jacob and established the law in Israel, and he commanded our forefathers to teach them to their children. For perpetuity God's ways will be passed down from one generation to the next, even to those not yet born. In this way, every generation will have a living faith in the laws of life and will never forget the faithful ways of God.* (Psalms 78:2-7 TPT).

TELL: I actually am going to expand this to "invite" someone from a different generation to coffee and ask them about their dreams and hopes.

CHAPTER 10

Be the Masterpiece Only You Can Be

"An original is worth more than a copy."

—Suzy Kassem

Strength, courage and audacity are a few of the character qualities that it takes to stand out in a crowd of imitations. Many copies, imitations and downright forgeries exist of our friend Mona Lisa, but not one of them come close to the value of the original. Being an original in a world that says blend in, imitate me, follow the status quo is our challenge and privilege. In a world of Insta-stars and Insta-celebrities that dictate everything from what to wear, what to eat, and what to think, the hard work of being the original God created is up to you.

Bonnie Ware, a caregiver for the terminally ill, spent time with people who were in the last 3-12 weeks of their lives. She realized the most important part of her job was not the physical care she gave to her patients, but her emotional support as she simply listened and heard the hearts cry of so many of those in her care.

On her blog bronnieware.com, she wrote about the top five regrets people have at the end of their life. The number one regret was, "I wish I'd had the courage to live a life true to myself, not the life others expected of me."

In the post *Regrets of the Dying* Ware said, "This was the most common regret of all. When people realize that their life is almost over and look back clearly on it, it is easy to see how many dreams have gone unfulfilled. Most people had not honored even a half of their dreams and had to die knowing that it was due to choices they had made, or not made. It is very important to try and honor at least some of your dreams along the way."

How hard is it to get to the end of our life and realize we have not fulfilled what God had designed for us to be and do? Everyone is given an allotment of time and what we do with that is up to each of us. Most importantly, not just what we do with it but how we choose to be who God has created us to be. How not to be the cheap imitations of what others want us to be, but to be our authentic and true selves.

For we are His workmanship [His own master work, a work of art], created in Christ Jesus [reborn from above—spiritually transformed, renewed, ready to be used] for good works, which God prepared [for us] beforehand [taking paths which He set], so that we would walk in

them [living the good life which He prearranged and made ready for us].
Ephesians 2:10 AMP (emphasis mine).

When Paul penned those words to the Ephesians, they would have
understood what he meant by the word "workmanship." Ephesus was a
thriving metropolis. Vision.org says, *"Ephesus was known throughout the
Roman world as the site of one of the Seven Wonders of the Ancient World,
the much-visited Temple of Artemis. Paul would have seen the temple as his
ship entered the estuary of the River Cayster and approached its harbor, which
had been specially dredged to accommodate sea traffic. Just to the north beyond
the dock stood the massive edifice—more than 400 feet long by 200 feet wide
(120 meters by 60 meters)—with its 127 marble columns, each nearly 60 feet,
or 18 meters, tall. Inside stood a statue of the fertility goddess, Artemis of the
Ephesians, possibly carved from a black meteorite (significant to the inhabitants
because it had fallen from the sky and was presumed to be a gift of the gods).
The idol's temple, which was four times the size of the Parthenon in Athens,
also served as a central bank and as a sanctuary for those accused of criminal
activity. Ephesus had all the problems of a wealthy port community."*

In Acts 19:21-34, we read about the great riot in the city of Ephesus
when Paul arrived and was teaching. The riot was caused by Apostle Paul
because, according to verse 26 he "had persuaded and turned a great
many people away saying that gods made with hands are not gods." This
upset a certain silversmith who earned his living creating "workmanships"
of Artemis. Almost every home had a "shrine" or a small replica of the
great Artemis in their home. This replica was reminder that she was to
be worshipped.

When Paul in Ephesians 2:10 said, that we are God's workmanship he
was saying that we are not a handmade replica of a dead god but divinely
made being created in His image. Created with purpose and on purpose.
Paul in his encouragement was telling the Ephesians, you are the replicas of
Jesus and you need to get out into the world and be on display.

When we embrace how much we are loved we can recognize the
fingerprints of God in our life. The experiences that shaped us, good or
bad, our personality with its strengths and weaknesses, and our unique
God-given potential all play a part in the "good works" God prepared

specifically for us. We must understand that even before we were conceived God had so many amazing plans for us. Plans that only you can fulfill with your unique self.

Living our authentic life is not about selfishness but about selflessness. In our attempt to hide, imitate or be someone other than our true selves we lose sight of what He wants for us and for those we are to influence in this life, whether we live to be 10 or 110.

I have come to appreciate who I am and who God has made me to be. This does not excuse me from growth and change, but it frees me to be about His business the way He made me. Honestly, it took me turning gray, in my twenties to love my red hair and freckles. It has taken me many more years to realize that my gift of encouragement, leadership and my need for it to be fun is all a part of God's plan for who he made me to be.

I may still be too loud, in my dress and in my mouth (I am still working on the latter) but I am more than just comfortable in who I am. I celebrate it. I want to bring as many people as God has called me to bring along on this journey as possible. To point others to my Master Artist, Jesus.

When we step into our Christ-centered identity the world is changed. The reason the enemy of our soul wants us to doubt whose we are is because we become ineffective. When we hide, when we imitate or we pretend that we are someone or something we are not, the world is missing out on YOU.

Fear of being discovered, kept Eve in hiding all the way back in the garden of Eden. As sons and daughters of Eve, we still deal with the fear of being discovered and in our hiding, we miss out on the rest of the story with its fairytale ending. The part of the story that is about our relationship with the one who loves us most.

We get to be a part of the best story ever told. We are at the very center of the great rescue. Rescued from who we thought we were; unloved, rejected and forgotten to the realization of being loved, accepted and chosen and adopted into the biggest and best family there is.

The thing about being His Masterpiece is we are forever marked. Historians have discovered in the very eye of the Mona Lisa are the master's initials. This masterpiece, the Mona Lisa took years to perfect, it is said that Leonardo Davinci started the painting her in Italy but finished her in France. The painting took four years to complete and Leonardo did not immediately share it with the world. What he was waiting for is not known, but what we know is that our master who is continually working on us wants us on display for all the world to see. Not because we are finished, but because we in our state of becoming who He wants us to be. We can model to the world that it is not about perfection or having arrived, but about the process of becoming.

A Work of Heart on Display

As you grow more into who you were meant to be, the more of God's confidence you will be able to personally grab a hold of. In her book *Daring Greatly,* Brene Brown talks about the need to be bravely you! To become the best version of you. The first step is becoming vulnerable to the one who created you. He knows you best anyway and if we try and hide from Him, we miss out on living an authentic and vulnerable life.

Brown says, "Vulnerability is the birthplace of love, belonging, joy, courage, empathy, and creativity. It is the source of hope, empathy, accountability, and authenticity. If we want greater clarity in our purpose or deeper and more meaningful spiritual lives, vulnerability is the path.

"So, we are convinced that every detail of our lives is continually woven together to fit into God's perfect plan of bringing good into our lives, for we are his lovers who have been called to fulfill his designed purpose" (Romans 8:28 TPT).

As we take small steps of vulnerability and courage, our story has the ability to change the lives of others. To give them freedom to be who they were created to be. The truth of Romans 8:28 comes into play more than ever, when we break the silence of who and what we are. We have each been called to fulfill His designed purpose.

ART

ASK: Now that I begin to see myself as a "masterpiece in the making," what is my next step to being on display for God? How can I begin/ continue in my journey of becoming His Masterpiece?

_____

_____

READ: *"Before I formed you in the womb I knew you [and approved of you as My chosen instrument], And before you were born I consecrated you [to Myself as My own]; I have appointed you as a prophet to the nations."* Then I said, *"Ah, Lord God! Behold, I do not know how to speak, For I am [only] a young man."* But the Lord said to me, *"Do not say, 'I am [only] a young man,' Because everywhere I send you, you shall go, and whatever I command you, you shall speak. "Do not be afraid of them [or their hostile faces], For I am with you [always] to protect you and deliver you,"* says the Lord. (Jeremiah 1:5-8 AMP)

TELL: This is your opportunity to allow others to see you as a masterpiece in progress. If you do not believe you are walking in your purpose, figure out where you can go and serve, or volunteer in an area you believe God has sculpted you for. Take time to learn what areas are available at your church or non-profit to be a part of. Or if you have the amazing privilege of your vocation being a place to expand into your purpose, take the risk and the time to make that happen.

APPENDIX A
Personality Profile Assessment*

1. In each of the rows of four words, place an X in front of the word that most often applies to you. Use the word definitions for the most accurate results. If you have trouble choosing between one or two words, check both-but no more than two words in each row. Place an X in front of the word (or words) on each line that most often applies to you.

2. Once you've finished transfer all your Xs to the corresponding words on the Personality Scoring Sheet and add up your totals. (Note: the words are in different order on the profile and scoring sheets)

3. Once you've transferred your answers to the scoring sheet, added up the totals in each of the four columns, and added the totals from both the strengths and weaknesses sections, you'll know your dominate personality type by the highest total number. You'll also see your secondary strength. Remember that everyone has a blend of two natural types. It will be normal to have a few Xs scattered in all four categories, but two personalities should come our strongest.

Strengths

1.	__Adventurous	__Adaptable	__Animated	__Analytical
2.	__Persistent	__Playful	__Persuasive	__Peaceful
3	__Submissive	__Self-sacrificing	__Sociable	__Strong-willed
4.	__Considerate	__Controlled	__Competitive	__Convincing
5.	__Refreshing	__Respectful	__Reserved	__Resourceful
6.	__Satisfied	__Sensitive	__Self-reliant	__Spirited
7.	__Planner	__Patient	__Positive	__Promoter
8.	__Sure	__Spontaneous	__Scheduled	__Shy
9.	__Orderly	__Obliging	__Outspoken	__Optimistic
10.	__Friendly	__Faithful	__Funny	__Forceful
11.	__Daring	__Delightful	__Diplomatic	__Detailed
12.	__Cheerful	__Consistent	__Cultured	__Confident
13.	__Idealistic	__Independent	__Inoffensive	__Inspiring
14.	__Demonstrative	__Decisive	__Dry humor	__Deep
15.	__Mediator	__Musical	__Mover	__Mixes easily
16.	__Thoughtful	__Tenacious	__Talker	__Tolerant
17.	__Listener	__Loyal	__Leader	__Lively
18.	__Contented	__Chief	__Chart maker	__Cute
19.	__Perfectionist	__Pleasant	__Productive	__ Popular
20.	__Bouncy	__Bold	__Behaved	__Balanced

Weaknesses

21.	__Blank	__Bashful	__Brassy	__Bossy
22.	__Undisciplined	__Unsympathetic	__Unenthusiastic	__Unforgiving
23.	__Reticent	__Resentful	__Resistant	__Repetitious
24.	__Fussy	__Fearful	__Forgetful	__Frank
25.	__Impatient	__Insecure	__Indecisive	__Interrupts
26.	__Unpopular	__Uninvolved	__Unpredictable	__Unaffectionate
27.	__Headstrong	__Haphazard	__Hard to please	__Hesitant
28.	__Plain	__Pessimistic	__Proud	__Permissive
29.	__Angered easily	__Aimless	__Argumentative	__Alienated
30.	__Naive	__Negative	__Nervy	__Nonchalant
31.	__Worrier	__Withdrawn	__Workaholic	__Wants credit
32.	__Too sensitive	__Tactless	__Timid	__Too talkative
33.	__Doubtful	__Disorganized	__Domineering	__Depressed
34.	__Inconsistent	__Introvert	__Intolerant	__Indifferent
35.	__Messy	__Moody	__Mumbles	__Manipulative
36.	__Slow	__Stubborn	__Short-tempered	__Scatterbrained
37.	__Loner	__Lords over others	__Lazy	__Loud
38.	__Sluggish	__Suspicious	__Short-tempered	__Scatterbrained
39.	__Revengeful	__Restless	__Reluctant	__Rash
40.	__Compromising	__Critical	__Crafty	__Changeable

Personality Scoring Sheet

Strengths

	Popular Sanguine	Powerful Choleric	Perfect Melancholy	Peaceful Phlegmatic
1.	__Animated	__Adventurous	__Analytical	__Adaptable
3.	__Playful	__Persuasive	__Persistent	__Peaceful
4.	__Sociable	__Strong-willed	__Self-sacrificing	__Submissive
5.	__Convincing	__Competitive	__Considerate	__Controlled
6.	__Refreshing	__Resourceful	__Respectful	__Reserved
7.	__Spirited	__Positive	__Planner	__Planner
8.	__Spontaneous	__Sure	__Scheduled	__Shy
9.	__Optimistic	__Outspoken	__Orderly	__Obliging
10.	__Funny	__Forceful	__Faithful	__Friendly
11.	__Delightful	__Daring	__Detailed	__Diplomatic
12.	__Cheerful	__Confident	__Cultured	__Consistent
13.	__Inspiring	__Independent	__Idealistic	__Inoffensive
14.	__Demonstrative	__Decisive	__Deep	__Dry Humor
15.	__Mixes easily	__Mover	__Musical	__Mediator
16.	__Talker	__Tenacious	__Thoughtful	__Tolerant
17.	__Lively	__Leader	__Loyal	__Listener
18.	__Cute	__Chief	__Chart maker	__Contented
19.	__Popular	__Productive	__Perfectionist	__Pleasant
20.	__Bouncy	__Bold	__Behaved	__Balanced
Total	_____	_____	_____	_____

	Popular Sanguine	Powerful Choleric	Perfect Melancholy	Peaceful Phlegmatic
21.	__Brassy	__Bossy	__Bashful	__Blank
22.	__Undisciplined	__Unsympathetic	__Unforgiving	__Unenthusiastic
23.	__Repetitious	__Resistant	__Resentful	__Reticent
24.	__Forgetful	__Frank	__Fussy	__Fearful
25.	__Interrupts	__Impatient	__Insecure	__Indecisive
26.	__Unpredictable	__Unaffectionate	__Unpopular	__Uninvolved
27.	__Haphazard	__Headstrong	__Hard to please	__Hesitant
28.	__Permissive	__Proud	__Pessimistic	__Plain
29.	__Angered easily	__Argumentative	__Alienated	__Aimless
30.	__Naive	__Nervy	__Negative attitude	__Nonchalant
31.	__Wants credit	__Workaholic	__Withdrawn	__Worrier
32.	__Talkative	__Tactless	__Too sensitive	__Timid
33.	__Disorganized	__Domineering	__Depressed	__Doubtful
34.	__Inconsistent	__Intolerant	__Introvert	__Indifferent
35.	__Messy	__Manipulative	__Moody	__Mumbles
36.	__Show-off	__Stubborn	__Skeptical	__Slow
37.	__Loud	__Lord over others	__Loner	__Lazy
38.	__Scatterbrained	__Short-tempered	__Suspicious	__Sluggish
39.	__Restless	__Rash	__Revengeful	__Reluctant
40.	__Changeable	__Crafty	__Critical	__Compromising
Total	_____	_____	_____	_____
Totals	_____	_____	_____	_____

APPENDIX B
Personality Profile
Word Definitions

1.

Adventurous. Takes on new and daring enterprises with a determination to master them.

Adaptable. Easily fits in and is comfortable in any situation.

Animated. Full of life, lively use of hands, arm and facial gestures.

Analytical. Likes to examine all the pieces for logical and proper relationships.

2.

Persistent. Sees one project through to its completion before starting another.

Playful. Full of fun and good humor.

Persuasive. Convinces through logic and fact rather than charm or power.

Peaceful. Seems undisturbed and tranquil and retreats from any form of strife.

Submissive. Easily accepts another's point of view or desire with little need to assert his or her own opinion.

Self-sacrificing. Willingly gives up own personal needs for the sake of or to meet the needs of others.

Sociable. Sees being with others as an opportunity to be cute and entertaining rather than as a challenge or business opportunity.

Strong-willed. Determined to have his or her own way.

Considerate. Has regard for the needs and feelings of others.

Controlled. Has emotional feelings but rarely displays them.

Competitive. Turns every situation, happening, or game into a contest and always plays to win!

Convincing. Can win someone over to anything through the sheer charm of his or her personality

5.

Refreshing. Renews, stimulates, or makes others feel good.

Respectful. Treats others with deference, honor, and esteem.

Reserved. Self-restrained in expression of emotion or enthusiasm.

Resourceful. Is able to act quickly and effectively in virtually all situations.

6.

Satisfied. Easily accepts any circumstance or situation.

Sensitive. Cares intensively about others and about what happens to them.

Self-reliant. Can fully rely on his or her own capabilities, judgment, and resources.

Spirited. Full of life and excitement.

7.

Planner. Prefers to work out a detailed arrangement beforehand for the accomplishment of a project or goal, and prefers involvement with the planning stages and the finished product rather than with carrying out the task.

Patient. Unmoved by delay, and remains calm and tolerant

Positive. Knows things will turn out right if he or she is in charge.

Promoter. Urges or compels others to go along, join in, or invest through the charm of personality

8.

Sure. Confident, rarely hesitates or wavers.

Spontaneous. Prefers all of life to be impulsive, unpremeditated activity, not restricted by plans.

Scheduled. Makes and lives by a daily plan, and dislikes when plans are interrupted.

Shy. Quiet, doesn't easily initiate a conversation.

9.

Orderly. Has a methodical, systematic arrangement of things.

Obliging. Accommodating, quick to do something another's way.

Outspoken. Speaks frankly and without reserve.

Optimistic. Sunny disposition, able to convince self and others that everything will turn out all right.

10.

Friendly. Responds rather than initiates, and seldom starts a conversation.

Faithful. Consistently reliable, steadfast, loyal and devoted, sometimes beyond reason.

Funny. Sparkling sense of humor that can make virtually any story into a hilarious event.

Forceful. A commanding personality against which others would hesitate to take a stand

11.

Daring. Willing to take risks; fearless, bold.

Delightful. Upbeat and fun to be with.

Diplomatic. Deals with people tactfully, sensitively, and patiently.

Detailed. Does everything in proper order with a clear memory of all the things that happen.

12.

Cheerful. Usually in good spirits, promotes happiness in others.

Consistent. Stays emotionally on an even keel, responding as others might expect.

Cultured. Interests involve both intellectual and artistic pursuits such as theater, symphony, or ballet.

Confident. Self- assured and certain of own ability and success

13.

Idealistic. Visualizes things in their perfect form and has a need to measure up to that standard.

Independent. Self-sufficient, self-supporting, self-confident, and seems to have little need of help.

Inoffensive. Never says or causes anything unpleasant or objectionable.

Inspiring. Encourages others to work, join, or be involved, and makes the whole thing fun.

14.

Demonstrative. Openly expresses emotion, especially affection, and doesn't hesitate to touch others while speaking to them.

Decisive. Quick and conclusive ability to make judgments.

Dry humor. Exhibits "dry wit," usually one-liners that can be sarcastic in nature.

Deep. Intense and often introspective with a distaste for surface conversation and pursuits.

15.

Mediator. Consistently taking the role of reconciling differences to avoid conflict.

Musical. Participates in or has a deep appreciation for music or is committed to music as an art form rather than for the fun of performing.

Mover. Is driven by a need to be productive, is a leader whom others follow and finds it difficult to sit still.

Mixes easily. Loves a party and can't wait to meet everyone in the room; never meets a stranger.

16.

Thoughtful. Considerate, remembers special occasions, and is quick to make a kind gesture.

Tenacious. Holds on firmly, stubbornly, and won't let go until the goal is accomplished.

Talker. Constantly talking, generally telling funny stories and entertaining everyone around; feels the need to fill the silence to make others comfortable.

Tolerant. Easily accepts the thoughts and ways of others without the need to disagree with or change them.

17.

Listener. Always seems willing to hear what others have to say.

Loyal. Faithful to a person, ideal, or job, sometimes beyond reason.

Leader. A natural director who is driven to be in charge and often finds it difficult to believe that anyone else can do the job as well.

Lively. Full of life, vigorous, and energetic.

18.

Contented. Easily satisfied with what he or she has, rarely envious.

Chief. Takes leadership and expects people to follow.

Chart maker. Organizes life, tasks, and problem solving by making lists, forms, or graphs.

Cute. Precious, adorable, center of attention.

19.

Perfectionist. Places high standards on self and often on others, desiring that everything be in proper order at all times.

Pleasant. Easygoing, easy to be around, easy to talk with.

Productive. Must constantly be working or achieving; often finds it very difficult to rest

Popular. Life of the party and therefore much desired as a party guest.

20.

Bouncy. A bubbly, lively personality, full of energy.

Bold. Fearless, daring, forward, unafraid of risk

Behaved. Consistently desires to conduct self within the realm of what seems proper.

Balanced. Stable, middle-of-the-road personality, not subject to sharp highs or lows

Weaknesses

21.

Blank. Shows little facial expression or emotion.

Bashful. Self-conscious, shrinks from getting attention.

Brassy. Showy, flashy, comes on strong, too loud.

Bossy. Commanding, domineering, sometimes overbearing in adult relationships.

22.

Undisciplined. Lack of order permeates most every area of his or her life.

Unsympathetic. Finds it difficult to relate to the problems or hurts of others.

Unenthusiastic. Tends not to get excited about anything, often feeling it won't work anyway.

Unforgiving. Has difficulty forgiving or forgetting a hurt or injustice; apt to hold a grudge.

23.

Reticent. Unwilling to get involved or struggles against involvement, especially when the situation is complex.

Resentful. Often holds ill feelings as a result of real or imagined offenses.

Resistant. Strives, works against, or hesitates to accept any other way but his or her own.

Repetitious. Retells stories and incidents to entertain without realizing he or she has already told the story several times before; constantly needs to say something.

24.

Fussy. Insistent about petty matters or details; calls for great attention to trivial details.

Fearful. Often experiences feelings of deep concern, apprehension, or anxiety.

Forgetful. Lack of memory, which is usually tied to a lack of discipline and not bothering to record mentally things that aren't fun.

Frank. Straightforward, outspoken, doesn't mind saying exactly what he or she thinks.

25.

Impatient. Finds it difficult to endure irritation or wait for others.

Insecure. Apprehensive or lacks confidence.

Indecisive. Finds it difficult to make any decision at all (not the personality that labors long over making decision to make the perfect one.)

Interrupts. More of a talker than a listener; starts speaking without even realizing someone else is already speaking.

26.

Unpopular. Intensity and demand for perfection can push others away.

Uninvolved. Has no desire to listen or become interested in clubs, groups, activities, or other people's lives.

Unpredictable. May be ecstatic one moment and down the next, or willing to help but then disappears, or promises to come but forgets to show up.

Unaffectionate. Finds it difficult to verbally or physically demonstrate tenderness.

27.

Headstrong. Insists on having his or her own way.

Haphazard. Has no consistent way of doing things.

Hard to please. Standards are set so high that it is difficult to ever be satisfied.

Hesitant. Slow to get moving and hard to get involved.

28.

Plain. A middle-of-the road personality with -out highs or lows and showing little, if any, emotion.

Pessimistic. While hoping for the best, generally sees the down side of a situation first.

Proud. Has great self-esteem and sees self as always right and the best person for the job.

Permissive. In an effort to be liked, allows others (including children) to do as they please.

29.

Angered easily. Has a childlike, flash-in-the-pan temper that expresses itself in tantrum style but is over and forgotten almost instantly.

Aimless. Not a goal setter, with little desire to be one.

Argumentative. Incites arguments, generally believing he or she is right no matter what the situation may be.

Alienated. Easily feels estranged from others, often because of insecurity or fear that others don't really enjoy his or her company.

30.

Naive. Simple and childlike perspective, lacking sophistication or comprehension of what the deeper levels of life are really about.

Negative Attitude. Attitude is seldom positive; often able to see only the down or dark side of each situation.

Nervy. Full of confidence, fortitude, and sheer guts, often in a negative sense.

Nonchalant. Easygoing, unconcerned, indifferent.

31.

Worrier. Consistently feels uncertain, troubled, or anxious.

Withdrawn. Pulls back and needs a great deal of alone or isolation time.

Workaholic. An aggressive goal setter who must be constantly productive and feels very guilty when resting, is not driven by a need for perfection or completion but by a need for accomplishment and reward.

Wants credit. Thrives on the credit or approval of others. As an entertainer feeds on the applause, laughter, and/or acceptance of an audience.

32.

Too sensitive. Overly introspective and easily offended when misunderstood.

Tactless. Sometimes expresses self in a some-what offensive and inconsiderate way.

Timid. Shrinks from difficult situations

Too talkative. An entertaining, compulsive talker who finds it difficult to listen.

33.

Doubtful. Characterized by uncertainty and lack of confidence that things will ever work out.

Disorganized. Lack of ability to ever get life in order.

Domineering. Compulsively takes control of situations and/or people, usually telling others what to do.

Depressed. Feels down much of the time.

34.

Inconsistent. Erratic, contradictory, with actions and emotions not based on logic.

Introvert. Thoughts and interests are directed inward; lives within self.

Intolerant. Appears unable to withstand or accept another's attitudes, point of view, or way of doing things.

Indifferent. Most things don't matter one way or the other.

35.

Messy. Living in a state of disorder, unable to find things.

Moody. Doesn't get very high emotionally, but slips easily into low lows, often when feeling unappreciated.

Mumbles. Talks quietly under his or her breath when pushed; doesn't bother to speak clearly.

Manipulative. Influences or manages shrewdly or deviously for own advantage; will get own way somehow.

36.

Slow. Often doesn't act or think quickly because it's too much of a bother.

Stubborn. Determined to exert own will, not easily persuaded, obstinate.

Show-off. Needs to be the center of attention; wants to be watched.

Skeptical. Disbelieving, questioning the motive behind the words.

37.

Loner. Requires a lot of private time and tends to avoid other people.

Lords over others. Doesn't hesitate to let others know that he or she is right or is in control.

Lazy. Evaluates work or activity in terms of how much energy it will take.

Loud. Laugh or voice can be heard above others in the room.

38.

Sluggish. Slow to get started; needs push to be motivated.

Suspicious. Tends to suspect or distrust others or their ideas.

Short-tempered. Has a demanding, impatience-based anger and a short fuse. Anger is expressed when others are not moving fast enough or have not completed what they have been asked to do.

Scatterbrained. Lacks the power of concentration or attention, flighty.

39.

Revengeful. Knowingly or otherwise holds a grudge and punishes the offender, often by subtly withholding friendship or affection.

Restless. Likes constant new activity because it isn't fun to do the same things all the time. Reluctant. Unwilling to get involved or struggles against it.

Reluctant. Unwilling to get involved or struggles against it.

Rash. May act hastily, without thinking things through, generally because of impatience.

40.

Compromising. Will often relax his or her position, even when right, to avoid conflict.

Critical. Constantly evaluating and making judgements, frequently thinking or expressing negative reactions.

Crafty. Shrewd; can always find a way to get to the desired end.

Changeable. A childlike, short attention span; need a lot of change and variety to keep from getting bored.

*Excerpt from *Wired That Way* by Florence and Marita Littauer, copyright 2006. Used by permission of Revell, a division of Baker Publishing Group

NOTES

Who Is the Master?
1. So Will I (100 Billion X) Words and Music by Joel Houston, Benjamin Hastings and Michael Fatkin, Wonder, Hillsong Music 2017

Intimacy, The Scariest Word.
1. McManus, Erwin. *Soul Cravings.* Thomas Nelson, 2006

Removing Barriers to Intimacy
1. Miller, Donald. *Scary Close; Dropping the Act and Finding True Intimacy.* Nelson Publishing, 2011
2. Thrall, Bill; McNichol, Bruce; Lynch, John. *True Faced. Trust God and others with who you are.* NavPress. 2003

What Medium Did the Master Use?
1. Warren, Rick. *Purpose Driven Life.* Zondervan. 2002
2. Mona Lisa, PAINTING BY LEONARDO DA VINCI, ENCYCOLOPEDIA BRITANNICA.COM
3. Littauer, Marita; Littauer Florence. *Wired That Way.* Revell. 2006

Purpose in the Pain
1. Austen, Jane. *Pride and Prejudice.* 1813

How Has the Master Molded Your Heart?

1. Welcome to Kibera, chaffinch.org.uk/kibera-slum/
2. Farrel, Pam. *Woman of Influence.* InterVarsity. 1996

Waiting for the Paint to Dry

1. Arizona127.Org for more information on Foster Care

Unveiling the Masterpiece

1. Winfery, Oprah *"O-Magazine"*

Be the Masterpiece Only You Can Be

1. Ware, Bronnie. *"Regrets of the Dying"* Bronnieware.com

Made in the USA
Monee, IL
01 February 2020